Be diligent
to present yourself
approved to God,

a worker who does not need
to be ashamed,

rightly dividing
the word of **truth.**

(2 Timothy 2:15)

Walking with the Victorious Warrior

Living the Christian Life

The second book in the Victorious Warrior Series

Jerry and Michelle Shelfer

Sebastopol, California
2025

WALKING WITH THE VICTORIOUS WARRIOR: *Living the Christian Life*
by Jerry and Michelle Shelfer
Copyright © 2025 Jerry and Michelle Shelfer
ISBN: 979-8-9897621-6-3

Capitalization has occasionally been modified from the original.
Definitions are from Noah Webster's 1828 *American Dictionary of the English Language*.

RaeLoch
PUBLISHING CO.

Dedication

We, your authors, have a story that started with our grievous sin of abortion. But that was only the beginning of our story. Jesus found us, and with His love and His mercy, He restored us beyond anything we could ever have imagined. By His wonderful grace, our family has grown now to include two children, thirteen grandchildren, and—through our ministry—countless spiritual sons and daughters worldwide. We pray that the information in this book goes forth to grow our spiritual family day by day and make young disciples among all nations. We dedicate this book to our wonderful youth leaders and their students who encounter Jesus through the Victorious Warrior program. May God richly bless you all as you live a life of study of the Scriptures and walk with the Victorious Warrior, Jesus.

Contents

For Parents, Teachers, and Leaders

THIS BOOK WAS WRITTEN AS A PRIMER to be used as a follow-on to our prior book, *The Victorious Warrior: Challenging Young People to Aim toward the Good*. It is the second in the Victorious Warrior series and is meant to answer the question, *Now that I've accepted Jesus Christ as my Savior, what does it mean to be a Christian?* While we have the youth reader in mind, it can be used as a general informative tool for new Christians of all ages.

This is what we believe: We preach "the gospel of Christ, for it is the power of God to salvation for everyone who believes."[1] "We believe in the One who raised Jesus our Lord from death. Jesus was handed over to die for our sins, and He was raised from death to make us right with God."[2] We present widely agreed-upon points of Christian understanding while leaving room for denominational differences on lesser points. In this, we seek to

---

[1] Romans 1:16, NEW KING JAMES VERSION (NKJV).

[2] Romans 4:24–25.

serve as many young Christians as we can. Our goal is to make disciples and help cultivate in them a burning desire to become learners about their faith. The readers are encouraged to explore all the topics further on their own or under the leadership of a good Bible teacher. We do not consider this primer exhaustive by any means but rather an invitation to go deeper. On our website, VictoriousWarrior.org, you will find additional materials for the teacher or for individual study.

Every point in this book is backed up with Scripture. We rely mostly on the Easy-to-Read Version for ease of understanding. Footnotes are numbered in a way that is meant to make the connection between verse and verse address as simple as possible to understand.

Additionally, we relied on Noah Webster's 1828 *American Dictionary of the English Language* for our definitions. Webster viewed language from a Christian worldview and therefore infused his definitions with a beautifully God-honoring sensibility.

We are convinced that the deeper Christians delve into the Bible and its riches, the more they will fall in love with the beauty, symmetry, grace, and holistic vision of the Savior's story. They will see the unity of the whole Bible—Old and New Testament together as "the whole counsel of God"—as a way to understand God and their own identity in His kingdom.

Jerry and Michelle Shelfer
Prepare a Room Ministries

Hello

... rightly dividing the word of truth ...

2 Timothy 2:15

First Steps

There was once a long-legged boy who met a curly-haired girl. They were two dim drifters who lost their way in life and made many poor choices together. If you have read *The Victorious Warrior: Challenging Young People to Aim toward the Good,* the first book in the Victorious Warrior series, you have already met them. These two just followed their desires, with no thought for the future or for consequences. They ignored the words of wisdom they had heard when they were younger about a loving and caring God who wanted the best for them.

Although they fell into a godless and wayward life, God was near and was patiently waiting for them to be ready to turn to Him. It was only after they went through terrible pain and loss from their poor choices that they finally had enough of themselves. That was the moment they turned and gave their lives to Jesus.

Once they began to live for Jesus, the long-legged boy and curly-haired girl realized they didn't know much about the Bible. They said to themselves, *Now that we are Christians, what does that mean? How are we to live? What now?*

What is it that Christians believe? Answering these questions became their daily challenge and joy, because as they read the Scriptures, they learned who God was and the plan He had for their lives. To them, the Bible became a wonderland of learning. Day by day, they grew in their faith and understanding.

> Now that we are Christians, what does that mean? How are we to live? What now? What is it that we believe?

As the years passed, these two became more and more aware that other young people were asking the very same questions they asked as young Christians. And so, this book was born. It comes from a desire to teach you, young Christians around the world, about your Christian faith and the message of the cross.

If you have not read *The Victorious Warrior: Challenging Young People to Aim toward the Good,* that is not a problem. The long-legged boy and curly-haired girl, your authors, still welcome you here!

We are so glad you picked up this book! Together, we are going to explore some very important topics—God and His plans for you. We hope this book challenges and encourages you to learn what it truly means to be a follower of Jesus. You have embarked on a wonderful new journey of discovery.

First, it is important that you have a Bible. You will need it for our studies together. You will also need something to write with. Grab your favorite pen or pencil. Don't be afraid to make notes or doodles in this book. There is space for you to write and questions to answer as you learn. Being diligent in your study of the Bible will help you become what the apostle Paul calls "one who does not need to be ashamed and who correctly explains the word of truth."[1]

---

[1] 2 Timothy 2:15, NEW LIVING TRANSLATION (NLT).

The lessons in this book are all supported by Bible verses. That is because the Bible is the final authority for what Christians believe. It is where you find the truth. For this reason, we quote it a lot. The chapters, verses, and Bible versions of the Scriptures we quote are found at the bottom of each page, identified by a number. If no Bible version is mentioned, that means the Scripture comes from the Easy-to-Read Version, which we really like because it is easy to understand.

For example, on page 2, look for the number 1 in a small rectangle at the very end of the last line of the page after the word "truth." Then, at the very bottom of the page under the gray line, you can see the number 1 in a small rectangle again, this time next to a Scripture address and a Bible version. That means that the quote, "one who does not need to be ashamed and who correctly explains the word of truth," is taken from the book of 2 Timothy, chapter 2 and verse 15, and that this quote is from the New Living Translation of the Bible, which from now on will be identified as NLT. The first time you see a new translation named, it will be spelled out. But after that, you will just see its initials.

> **The word *disciple* means "learner." We want you to be a disciple of Jesus—one who is devoted to learning all about Him.**

We hope you are going through this book in a group setting so you can have lively discussions with other Christians about what you are learning. Speaking and hearing what others have to say helps to increase your understanding. Also, don't be afraid to ask questions. Your questions may help others who are too afraid to ask.

The first disciples of Jesus were men and women who followed Him when He was on earth. The word *disciple* means "learner." We want you to be a disciple of Jesus—one who is devoted to learning all about Him—and to find all the joy that comes from being His disciple. He has much to teach you, as He says, "so that you will be filled with My joy. Yes, your joy will overflow!"[2]

"Like newborn babies hungry for milk, you should want the pure teaching that feeds your spirit."[3] Just as a baby starts out with milk and moves to solid food, so it is with learning about God's truths in the Bible. God will guide you to ever greater and deeper understanding of His Word. You will go from spiritual milk to spiritual meat. *Bring a good appetite!*

MORE TO DISCUSS:

---

[2] John 15:11, NLT.

[3] 1 Peter 2:2.

1.   Take your Bible out and look at the title page. Find where it says the version of your Bible. Some examples of popular versions in English are the King James Version (KJV), New Living Translation (NLT), and New International Version (NIV). The different versions are various translations from the original written languages of the Bible. Even though they use slightly different words, the meaning is mostly the same. Sometimes, reading different versions of Bible verses can help us better understand the meaning.

2.   Now, go to Psalm 23 and read it in your Bible. If possible, find a friend, teacher, or someone in your group who uses a different version of the Bible from yours. Have that person read Psalm 23 too. Notice how the words of the psalm are slightly different, yet the meaning is the same. Write down what you noticed by doing this little comparison of Bible translations.

3.   What does it mean to you to be a "learner"?

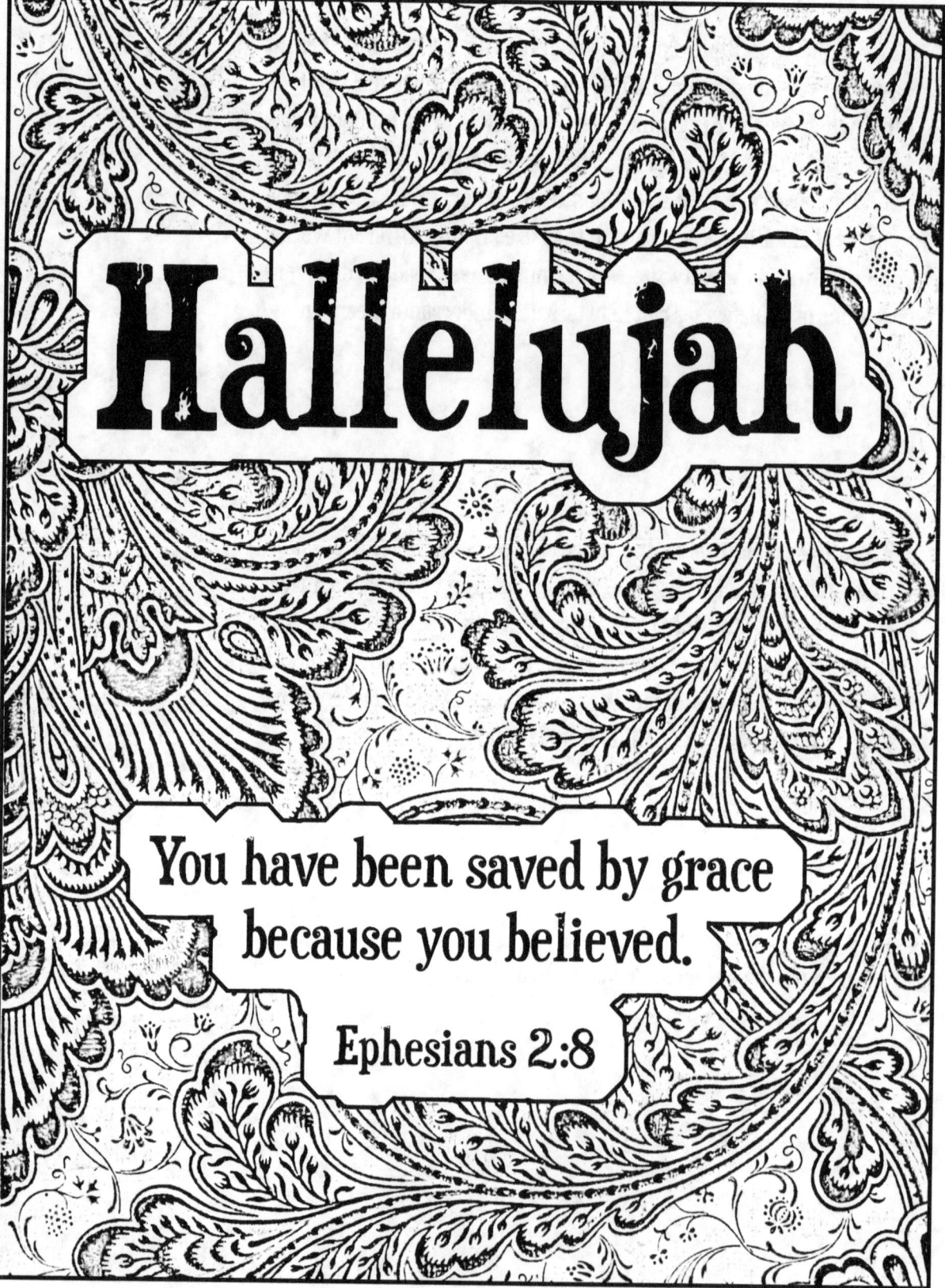

1 • A Hallelujah Welcome!

The LORD your God is in your midst, a Victorious Warrior. He will rejoice over you with joy. [1]

As a new Christian, you have reached a very important moment in your life. You have become a follower of Jesus, the Victorious Warrior who won the Great Battle between good and evil and defeated sin and death. You have turned away from your selfish and me-centered life and turned instead toward the One who made you and loves you. The angels are even now joining the Victorious Warrior, Jesus, in rejoicing over you with shouts of hallelujah! Jesus Himself said, "I tell you, there is joy in the presence of the angels of God over one sinner who repents." [2]

---

[1] Zephaniah 3:17, NEW AMERICAN STANDARD BIBLE (NASB).

[2] Luke 15:10, NASB.

God met your tiny bit of faith with His immeasurable grace and gave salvation to you as a free gift. "If you openly say, 'Jesus is Lord' and believe in your heart that God raised Him from death, you will be saved."[3] "You have been saved by grace because you believed. You did not save yourselves; it was a gift from God."[4]

> **There is joy in the presence of the angels of God over one sinner who repents.**

People come to be Christians in many ways. The Holy Spirit of God knew exactly how to speak to each one in his or her own language, and He knew how to speak to you too. You may have accepted Christ after taking the Victorious Warrior course. Maybe you heard something about Jesus on the internet and found Him that way. You may have had a miraculous personal encounter with Jesus, or you may have just felt His presence in a quiet way. Maybe you accepted Christ while attending a church service. Or maybe someone took the time to speak to you one-on-one and share the gospel. Everyone's story of being found by Jesus is unique and precious. But no matter how you got here, we want you to go deeper in your understanding of what it means to be a follower of Jesus Christ.

What is your story? How did you come to accept Jesus Christ as your Savior?

_____

_____

_____

_____

_____

[3] Romans 10:9.

[4] Ephesians 2:8.

8

YOU ARE A NEW PERSON

Sin equals death. "When people sin, they earn what sin pays—death. But God gives His people a free gift—eternal life in Christ Jesus our Lord."[5] When you accepted Jesus, all your sin was forgiven, so you have been given life instead of death. "Anyone who belongs to Christ has become a new person. The old life is gone; a new life has begun!"[6] You can now look forward to eternal life as a new person with God.

> **Sin:** To depart voluntarily from the path of duty prescribed by God.

What does it mean to become a new person? It means that you have been spiritually cleansed, and now you no longer have to carry guilt and shame for your sin. Instead, you can have joy and freedom. You are living a new life

> **What does it mean to become a new person? It means that you have been spiritually cleansed.**

[5] Romans 6:23.

[6] 2 Corinthians 5:17, NLT.

9

with Jesus. Naturally, you will not want to treat God's enormous grace toward you as something to be toyed with by continuing to sin. With the help of God's Holy Spirit, you will be filled with a desire to please God with your thoughts and actions. From here on, you will start to look at the world with new eyes, understanding it through the words of the Bible. As the Holy Spirit gives you understanding, you will more and more align your life with God's plan. The Bible will guide you and lay a foundation for you to "have life and have it abundantly."[7]

According to the Bible, what happened to you when you accepted Jesus?

_____

_____

_____

_____

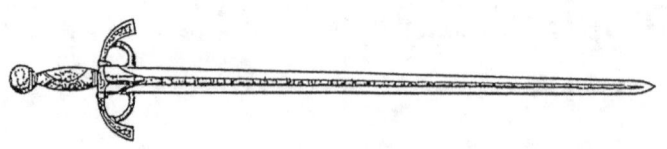

---

[7] John 10:10, ENGLISH STANDARD VERSION (ESV).

YOUR ABUNDANT LIFE

What is the meaning of the word *abundant*? It means having an overflow that makes you content and satisfied—it is more than enough. This abundant life is the life that Jesus has for you as a Christian. The abundant life Jesus promises is not one of riches, fine clothes, fancy cars, or fame. Those are things of the physical world.

> **The abundant life that Jesus has for you is about the riches of the spiritual world—abundance that no money can buy.**

Instead, the abundant life that Jesus has for you is about the riches of the spiritual world—abundance that no money can buy. The abundance Jesus has for you is a sense of His presence with you wherever you go. It is peace and joy. It is His love for you assuring you every day that you are cherished. It is His help in overcoming addictions and failings so that you can live free. It is the quiet assurance that you are walking with the One who

> **Abundant:** Plentiful; in great quantity; fully sufficient; overflowing.

is your help in times of trouble and never leaves your side. It is the confidence that when you die, you have everlasting life with God. As Jesus prayed to the Father, "This is the way to have eternal life—to know You, the only true God, and Jesus Christ, the one You sent to earth."[8]

The abundant life Jesus has for you does not mean your life won't be difficult or that you won't face all the challenges that every human being goes through. But God is able to use even your hard times to mature, shape, and mold you into the person He wants you to be.

The abundant life God has for you will become a beautiful way for God's love to shine through you. It will be visible to the people around you, leading them to ask, "Where did you get that peace and joy? I want that too!" That will give you the chance to be an ambassador for Christ and invite others to enjoy the abundant life Jesus has for them.

Fill in the columns under the two headings below with examples of abundant life according to the physical and spiritual worlds:

Abundant Life according to the Physical World	Abundant Life according to the Spiritual World

[8] John 17:3, NLT.

YOUR GUIDEBOOK, THE BIBLE

Every day, as you read the Bible—your new guidebook to life—you will find nuggets of wisdom, comfort, and guidance that will seem to be written just for you and your unique circumstances. For this reason, the Bible is sometimes called a "living book" because of its special way of speaking to you with just the right words at the exact moment you need to hear them.

> **The Bible is sometimes called a "living book" because of its special way of speaking with just the right words at the exact moment you need to hear them.**

Just when someone abuses you for your newfound faith in Jesus, you happen to read Jesus's assuring words, "People will insult you and hurt you. They will lie and say all kinds of evil things about you because you follow Me. But when they do that, know that great blessings belong to you. Be happy about it. Be very glad because you have a great reward waiting for you in heaven. People did these same bad things to the prophets who lived before you."[9]

Just when you wonder if God really sees and cares about your hard life, you happen to read this reminder

---

[9] Matthew 5:11–12.

from the apostle Peter: "Give all your worries to Him, because He cares for you."[10]

Just when you doubt whether Jesus could ever really desire to be with that flawed person you see in the mirror, you come across Jesus's prayer to Father God: "Father, I want these people You have given Me to be with Me in every place I am. I want them to see My glory—the glory You gave Me because You loved Me before the world was made."[11]

And the more you read the Bible, the more you will find these powerful insights and assurances. Your faith will grow day by day. You will start to notice yourself changing. Those around you might even notice a change in you.

You may wake up each morning with the same physical needs and challenges—you splash water on your face, dress, go to school or work, deal with people throughout the day, and do many of the same things you did before. At the end of each day, you lay your head on the same pillow. But now, you are steadily gaining knowledge and growing spiritually.

Ever since Moses wrote the first five books of the Bible some three thousand years ago, people have been studying the Bible. The Bible authors who came after Moses studied what Moses wrote, and the later Bible authors studied what the earlier Bible authors wrote, as we see in their writings. And people have continued to study it in every generation. It is a book that speaks to all people of all time periods, and it speaks to you too.

Have you ever read or heard passages from the Bible that spoke directly to what you were going through? Describe.

_____

_____

_____

_____

---

[10] 1 Peter 5:7.

[11] John 17:24.

YOU ARE BORN AGAIN

Before you became a Christian, you may have thought you were alive, and physically, you were. But "in the past you were spiritually dead because of your sins and the things you did against God."[12] You were chasing after pleasures and things of the flesh rather than things of the spirit.

> # At the very moment when you gave your life to Jesus, something extraordinary happened.

At the very moment when you gave your life to Jesus, something extraordinary happened. You became spiritually alive—transformed into a new being. You were *born again*, not in a way that would mean returning to your mother's belly but a new birth into the spiritual life. You became a citizen of God's heavenly kingdom. Jesus describes the change this way: "The only life people get from their human parents is physical. But the new life that the Spirit gives a person is spiritual. Don't be surprised that I told you, 'You must be born again.'"[13]

By the work of the Holy Spirit, the Lord drew you to Himself, and He did this in a way that was unique to you, by appealing to you in a way you understood. He reaches each person in his or her own way. For example,

---

[12] Ephesians 2:1.

[13] John 3:6–7.

He may reach an emotional person through their emotions. Or, He may reach a studious person through rational thought.

Now that you are born again, your mind has shifted its focus from things of the flesh and of the world to things of the spirit. You are "made new in your hearts and in your thinking."[14]

Becoming a new person doesn't mean you stop being yourself. Instead, it means you are on a path to becoming the best possible version of yourself. Now, all that you do has a high purpose—that purpose is to be in God's presence, enjoy Him, and glorify Him—to "stand before Him without any fault."[15] Your life is to be a reflection to the world of the beauty, holiness, and love of God.

When you believed, you received the gift of the Holy Spirit. "In Christ, God put His special mark on you by giving you the Holy Spirit that He promised."[16] What exactly is the Holy Spirit doing? The Holy Spirit is cleaning you from the inside out, "according to His mercy, by the washing of regeneration and renewing by the Holy Spirit."[17]

When you believed, you were made holy and able to come into God's presence. The voice of the Holy Spirit in you is prompting you to become more

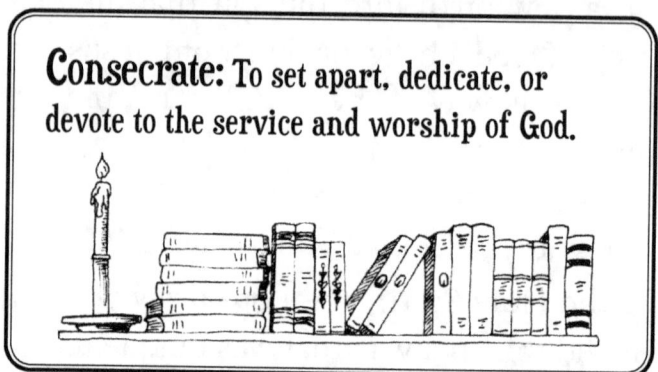

Consecrate: To set apart, dedicate, or devote to the service and worship of God.

14 Ephesians 4:23.

15 Ephesians 1:4.

16 Ephesians 1:13.

17 Titus 3:5, NASB.

and more like Jesus every day—that is, He is consecrating you. *Consecrated* means to be made holy, or set apart for God's purposes, like a vessel of honor in God's great mansion. "If anyone cleanses himself from what is dishonorable, he will be a vessel for honorable use, set apart as holy, useful to the master of the house, ready for every good work." [18]

What are some things you used to do that you no longer want to do because of the work of the Holy Spirit consecrating you?

_____

_____

_____

_____

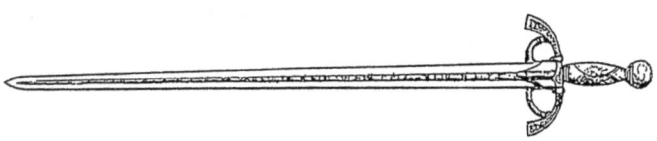

[18] 2 Timothy 2:21, ESV.

YOUR GOOD NEWS

Another word for "good news" in the Bible is *gospel*. What exactly is this gospel? It is best summarized by these words of Jesus: "Yes, God loved the world so much that He gave His only Son, so that everyone who believes in Him would not be lost but have eternal life."[19] God became man. That man lived among us. That man died for our sins. Then He rose from the dead. And now, everyone who believes in Him can be free of their sin and have eternal life with Him. That is the gospel.

Before you were saved, you were spiritually dead in your sins. The Bible says, "All have sinned and are not good enough to share God's divine greatness. They are made right with God *by His grace*. This is a free gift. They are made right with God by being made free from sin through Jesus Christ."[20]

The gospel of Jesus Christ "is the power God uses to save everyone who believes."[21] When you heard the gospel, or good news, of Jesus's free offer of salvation and you believed, you were saved, by the grace of God. What is God's grace? It is the kind and merciful work of God, freely given. It is undeserved, or unmerited. This means it is not given to you based on your merit, or how good you are. God's grace is not at all based on anything you did or did not do. It is purely a gift that shows God's love, mercy, and care for you.

This is such a beautiful reason to worship your loving and merciful God and to take the attention off yourself and put it onto

> **God's grace is not at all based on anything you did or did not do. It is purely a gift that shows God's love, mercy, and care for you.**

---

[19] John 3:16.

[20] Romans 3:23–24.

[21] Romans 1:16.

Him—the one who deserves all your praise! Anytime you catch yourself taking the credit for your blessings, success, or circumstances, remember that "everything good comes from God. Every perfect gift is from Him. These good gifts come down from the Father who made all the lights in the sky."[22]

> **Grace:** The free unmerited love and favor of God, the spring and source of all the benefits men receive from Him.

The grace of God not only saves us but also helps us to live right. "For the grace of God that brings salvation has appeared to all men, teaching us that, denying ungodliness and worldly lusts, we should live soberly, righteously, and godly in the present age."[23]

When you stop and take a moment to think of all the blessings of your life—even seemingly little things like waking up this morning, having air to breathe, or being able to use your mind—you can't help but see that these blessings *all* come to you by the grace of God. By the grace of God, I was not struck by a car on my way home today. By the grace of God, I have enough money to buy the clothes I need. By the grace of God, I found my lost

---

[22] James 1:17.

[23] Titus 2:11–12, NEW KING JAMES VERSION (NKJV).

keys. Every good thing that happens to you is because God is gracious, is merciful, and loves you.

Can you imagine that even when your life gets rough, you might see God's grace in it? The apostle Paul had a serious problem and prayed to God three times for Him to remove the problem. But God did not remove it. Instead, "the Lord said, 'My grace is all you need.'"[24]

Are you ever tempted to boast about the good things you do? Memorize this important Scripture that speaks of God's grace, in any version. Here is one you might use:

"You have been saved by grace because you believed. You did not save yourselves; it was a gift from God. You are not saved by the things you have done, so there is nothing to boast about."[25]

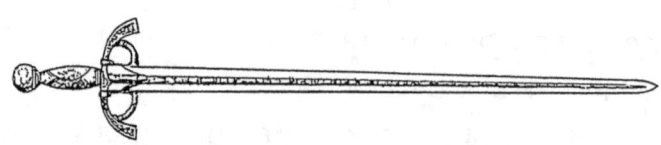

---

[24] 2 Corinthians 12:9.

[25] Ephesians 2:8–9.

YOUR NEW FAMILY

As a follower of Jesus Christ, you are now part of a great community of believers. In fact, you can even think of them as brothers and sisters in your new family. You have a family by blood, and now you have a new family by the Spirit. "God provides homes for those who are lonely."[26] Most Christians gather together on Sundays to worship God and celebrate our shared salvation as a family. This is part of what makes life in Christ meaningful. This new family gives you a sense of belonging and a chance to make new friends who are on the same path as you.

Your local community of believers is where you will also find mentors to guide you, teachers to help you understand the Bible, chances to serve and love others, and joyful fellowship with like-minded Christians who will help you on your path. It can be a community made up of very different types of people, all joined together by their love for Jesus. You have much to learn from those who have been walking with Jesus longer than you. And one day, you, too, will be a mature Christian helping others new to the faith.

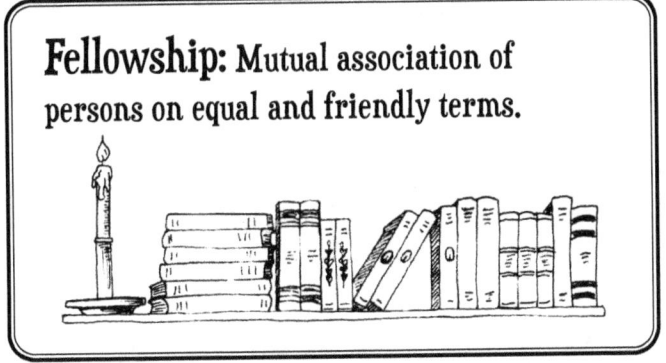

Fellowship: Mutual association of persons on equal and friendly terms.

---

26 Psalm 68:6.

You will also be challenged to stretch beyond your comfort zone and become friends with people you may not have chosen for yourself. In heaven, you will see God has chosen a rainbow of people from all over the world to dwell together with Him. The Bible puts it this way: "Now, in Christ, it doesn't matter if you are a Jew or a Greek, a slave or free, male or female. You are all the same in Christ Jesus."[27] Your common faith in Jesus is all that matters. Be open to others even if that means crossing cultural, economic, tribal, racial, ethnic, age, or national divides. God's believers come in all shapes, sizes, and colors, and Jesus places a very high value on the unity of His believers. "You are citizens together with God's holy people. You belong to God's family."[28]

As a new Christian, you may have many questions about what Christians believe and why. In the next section, you will find answers to some basic questions about what it means to follow Jesus.

> **Before you were born again, you may have been uncomfortable with certain groups of people. Now that you are born again, are you ready to see all believers as your brothers and sisters in Christ, regardless of race, tribe, nationality, clan, or any other differences? If not, pray that the Holy Spirit of God would help you to see others with God's eyes of love. Discuss.**

_____

_____

_____

_____

_____

27 Galatians 3:28.

28 Ephesians 2:19.

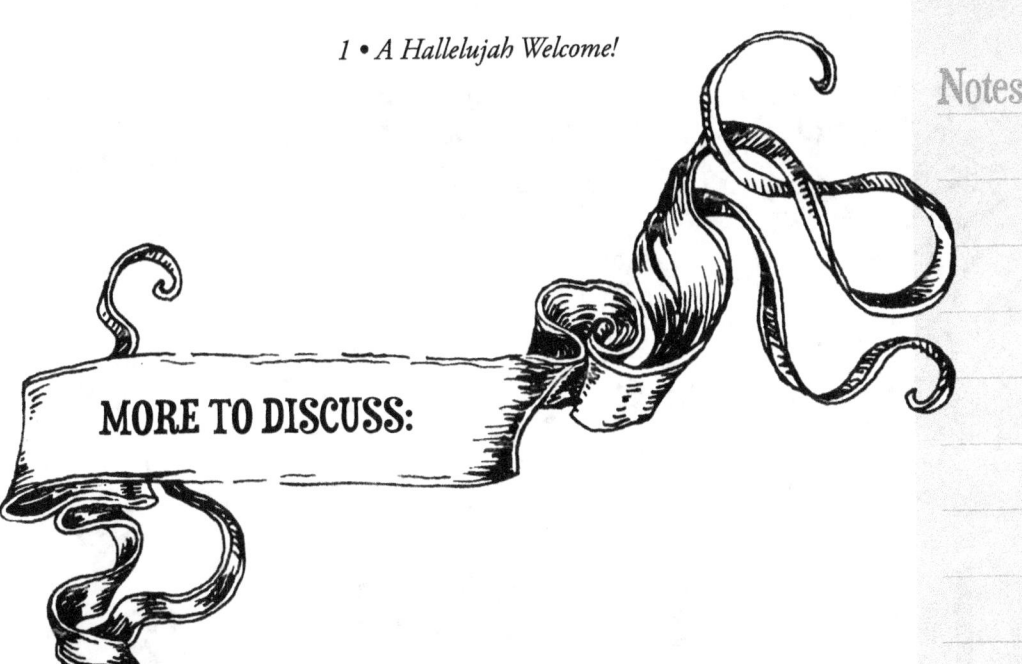

MORE TO DISCUSS:

1. You are a new person in Christ. How have you seen yourself change since you were born again?

2. What would you say about your new life to a friend who does not know Jesus?

3. Gathering together with other Christians helps strengthen your faith. Have you found a church or community to be a part of?

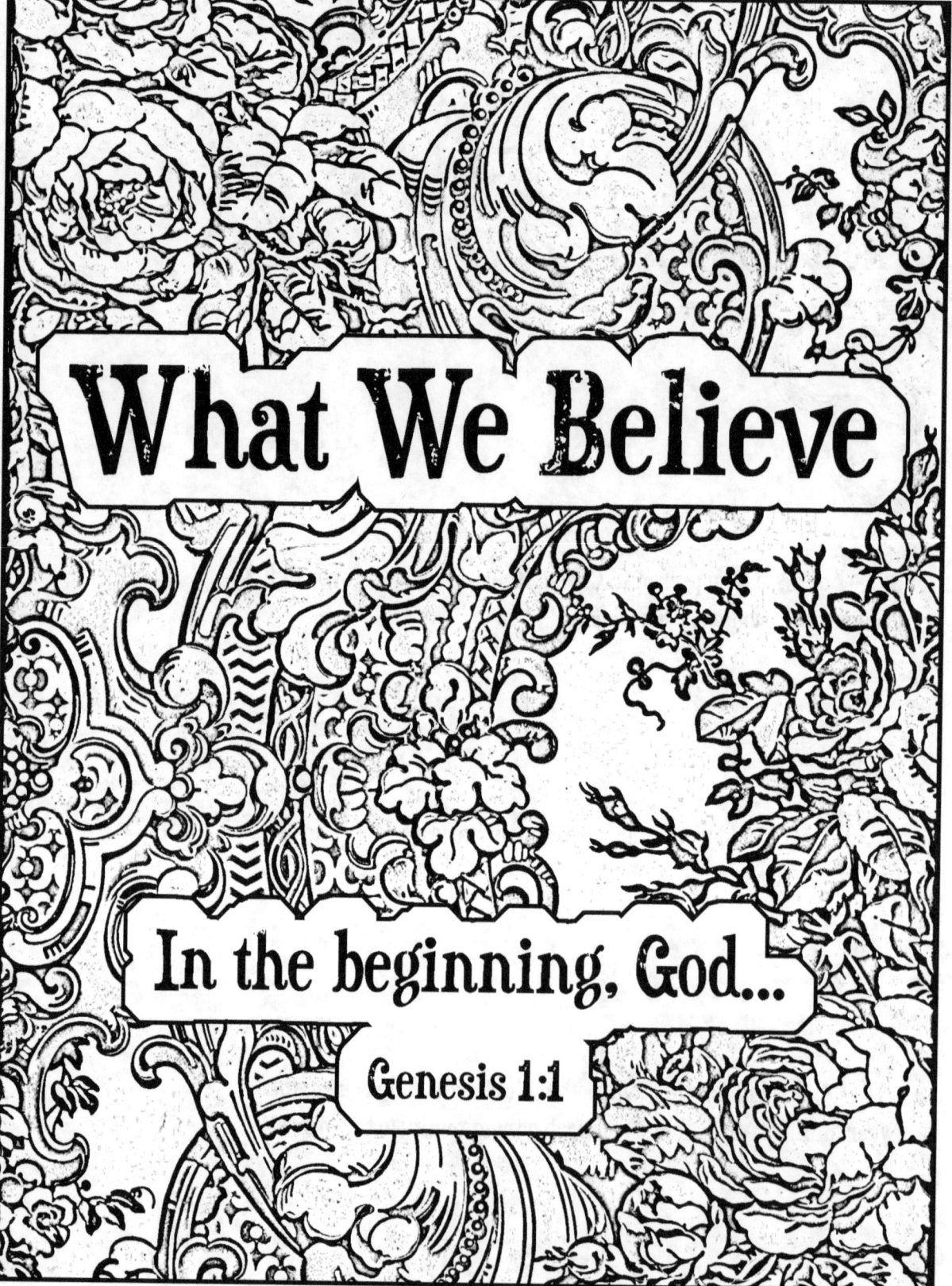

What We Believe

In the beginning, God...

Genesis 1:1

2 • What We Believe

In this section, we will explore the basic beliefs of the Christian faith. Like the long-legged boy and the curly-haired girl, you may have come to Jesus without knowing much about the Bible or the Christian life. But that is not where you want to stay. With your Bible in your hand, you can explore a world of knowledge like many who came before you and like millions of Christians around the world who are studying the Bible even now. Welcome to a wonderful journey of discovery!

The lessons you will find in this section are based on generally accepted Christian teachings. Use them as a starting point in your studies. We hope that you refer to these lessons often. Let's start with the first things first: *Who is God?*

WHO IS GOD?

Who is this being we call God? Who is this One we dedicate our lives to when we become Christians? Who is the One in whom we place our hopes for an abundant life, freedom from sin, and a glorious eternity? Who is it that we worship and pray to?

The answer to these questions can be found in the Holy Bible. That is where God chose to reveal Himself to us. There, we learn that God is an all-powerful being who created the universe and everything in it. The very first words of the Bible declare, "In the beginning God created the heavens and the earth."[1] The universe is physical and exists in time and space. God, who created the universe, exists outside of and apart from His creation, time, and space. In the same way that the potter forms the clay pot but *is not* the clay pot, God formed the universe but *is not* the universe. God was never created. He has always existed and always will exist. He has no beginning and no end. That's hard for us to understand, but it is so!

> In the same way that the potter forms the clay pot but *is not* the clay pot, God formed the universe but *is not* the universe.

Some people who are not Christians may use the word *god* to describe many different beings and ideas, but the Bible clearly tells us there is only one true God, and He says of Himself, "I am the only God, the one who does what is right. I am the one who saves, and there is no other!"[2]

The greatest scholars and thinkers can study their whole lives and never fully understand all that God is. He is beyond our understanding. He tells us, "My thoughts are not like yours. Your ways are not like Mine. Just as

---

[1] Genesis 1:1, NLT.

[2] Isaiah 45:21.

the heavens are higher than the earth, so My ways are higher than your ways, and My thoughts are higher than your thoughts."[3]

At the same time, God wants us to know Him. He wants to reveal His character to us, and He uses the Bible to do so. Also, just as an artist shows his character in the art he creates, so God reveals His character in His magnificent creation. "For ever since the world was created, people have seen the earth and sky. Through everything God made, they can clearly see His invisible qualities—His eternal power and divine nature."[4] When we study nature and read the Bible, we get to know God. The following are some qualities of God, but remember that He has no limit and is much more than this:

God is omnipotent, or all-powerful. That means God can do all things. "Greatness, power, glory, victory, and honor belong to You, because everything in heaven and on earth belongs to You!"[5]

Inscrutable: That cannot be penetrated, discovered or understood by human reason.

---

[3] Isaiah 55:8–9.

[4] Romans 1:20, NLT.

[5] 1 Chronicles 29:11.

God is omniscient, or all-knowing. That means God knows everything and nothing is hidden from His sight. "Oh, the depth of the riches and wisdom and knowledge of God! How unsearchable are His judgments and how inscrutable His ways!"[6]

God is omnipresent. That means God is everywhere at once. He is not limited to time, space, or any physical laws. "Your Spirit is everywhere I go. I cannot escape Your presence. If I go up to heaven, You will be there. If I go down to the place of death, You will be there. If I go east where the sun rises or go to live in the west beyond the sea, even there You will take my hand and lead me. Your strong right hand will protect me."[7]

God is holy. That means He is set apart from all else, and He is righteous, just, and perfect in all His ways and judgments. "I am the LORD your God. I am holy."[8]

God is sovereign. That means that He does what He wants to do at His pleasure. "He does as He pleases among the angels of heaven and among the people of the earth."[9] "The LORD does whatever He wants, in heaven and on earth, in the seas and the deep oceans."[10] And because all His judgments are perfect, what He does is always right, even if we don't understand it.

God is good. That means that everything about God meets the highest standard of quality. But God is not just good—He is the Author of goodness. He is the one who defined right and wrong, good and evil to begin with. Without His moral standard, we would not know the difference between good and evil. He is the one who placed that moral compass within each of us so that we can know what is good and recognize Him. God is not just good—God is infinitely good. Those who reject God also reject His standards of goodness,

---

[6] Romans 11:33, ESV.

[7] Psalm 139:7–10.

[8] Leviticus 19:2.

[9] Daniel 4:35, NLT.

[10] Psalm 135:6.

making it allowable in their eyes to do all sorts of evil things. But we who follow God seek after goodness in our own lives. "The LORD is good! There is no end to His faithful love. We can trust Him forever and ever!"[11] "Taste and see that the LORD is good. Oh, the joys of those who take refuge in Him!"[12]

God is love. That means that God's nature is love. "God is love. Everyone who lives in love lives in God, and God lives in them."[13] Just as God shows infinite goodness, He radiates infinite love. He is the Author of love. His love is not imperfect like human love. It shows itself in His willingness to sacrifice His Son to save us from our sins. Jesus teaches that "the greatest love people can show is to die for their friends,"[14] and that is exactly what Jesus did for us.

What are three other words that describe God? Write them here.

_____

_____

_____

This is a first glimpse at who God is. Now, we will look at a very mysterious quality of God—He is three persons in one.

---

[11] Psalm 100:5.

[12] Psalm 34:8, NLT.

[13] 1 John 4:16.

[14] John 15:13.

WHAT IS THE TRINITY?

One part of God's nature needs some explanation. God is one that exists in three persons—that is, He is one God in the form of a Trinity. He is God the Father, God the Son, and God the Holy Spirit, and yet He is one God. This is a mystery. One way of thinking of the Trinity that makes sense is to think of it as a mathematical equation. We might think it makes sense to add one plus one plus one to equal three, but God cannot be contained in such numbers. Instead, add infinity plus infinity plus infinity. The result? Infinity! Infinity times infinity times infinity also equals infinity! And there can only be one infinity. When we understand the infinite nature of God, then the equation of three in one can make perfect sense.

The three persons of the Trinity have existed and will exist together as one from everlasting to everlasting. All three have the same plan and purpose because they are one. They never contradict. They have a loving and harmonious relationship. They are three in one. The Trinity is also sometimes referred to as the Godhead.

Let's look more closely at the three persons of the Trinity and how they work together.

> They never contradict. They have a loving and harmonious relationship. They are three in one.

God the Father

God the Father is spirit. "God is spirit. So the people who worship Him must worship in spirit and truth."[15] He is invisible. "No one has ever seen God."[16] Yet God reveals Himself in many ways. He reveals Himself through the words of the Bible, His creation, His Son, Jesus, the Holy Spirit, and other believers. The Father is the One who sent the Son and the Spirit to us. "God

---

[15] John 4:24.

[16] John 1:18.

sent His Son into the world."[17] Jesus says of the Spirit, "This Helper is the Holy Spirit that the Father will *send* in My name."[18] In this last verse, we clearly see all three persons of the Trinity: the Father sends the Spirit in the name of the Son.

Even though God is invisible and may seem far away, He is really very involved and cares about every detail of our lives. He is compassionate, slow to anger, merciful, and loving. He is not remote or distant. He is not cruel. He is like a good father, protecting and providing for us.

List five qualities of a good father.

_____

_____

_____

_____

God the Son

God the Son is also God, yet He is not another god. He is the same God in a different person. The Son, Jesus, "was like God in every way."[19] "The Son shows the glory of God. He is a perfect copy of God's nature."[20] He took the form of a man (or "manifested") and came to live among us. He was fully man and fully God at the same

---

[17] John 3:17.

[18] John 14:26.

[19] Philippians 2:6.

[20] Hebrews 1:3.

time. He was born to the virgin Mary, lived a sinless life, and died a horrible death on a cross, all because of His great love for us.

Manifested: Made clear; disclosed; made apparent, obvious or evident.

The blood Jesus shed on the cross has the power to cleanse us from our sins. He makes us holy so we can be in the presence of a holy God. He willingly shed His blood and allowed His body to be broken so that our sins would not keep us from being with God.

After He died, Jesus rose from the dead. This gives us everlasting life with Him. When His first mission was complete here on earth, God the Son went up to heaven and is now sitting at the right hand of God the Father. But He is returning one day as a conquering king, and His reign will be without end. That will be a glorious day!

> # He is returning one day as a conquering king, and His reign will be without end. That will be a glorious day!

When God speaks things into existence, it is through the work of the Son. "Everything was made through Him, and nothing was made without Him." [21]

---

[21] John 1:3.

"Through His power all things were made."[22] Because Jesus brings into existence what the Father speaks, Jesus is called the Word of God. "Before the world began, the Word was there. The Word was with God, and the Word was God …. The Word became a man and lived among us."[23]

Jesus, the Word that "became a man," showed us who God is in a way that people could see, touch, hear, and talk to when He was here on earth. One of Jesus's disciples said, "We want to tell you about the Word that gives life—the one who existed before the world began. This is the one we have heard and have seen with our own eyes. We saw what He did, and our hands touched Him."[24]

Jesus says:

"I am not trying to please Myself. I want only to please the One who sent Me."[25]

What does this tell us about the relationship between the Father and the Son?

_____

_____

_____

_____

_____

[22] Colossians 1:16.

[23] John 1:1, 14.

[24] 1 John 1:1.

[25] John 5:30.

God the Holy Spirit

God the Holy Spirit is also God. The Holy Spirit was present at the creation of the universe. "God's Spirit moved over the water."[26] In the original language of Genesis (Hebrew), the word for Spirit also means "wind" and "breath." The Holy Spirit is the breath that gave life to Adam and still gives life to all living things. The Spirit is the one that made Mary pregnant with baby Jesus. An angel told her, "The Holy Spirit will come to you, and the power of the Most High God will cover you."[27] Just as the Holy Spirit brought order out of chaos when He hovered over the waters at creation, and He brought life to Mary's womb, He brings order and life to our lives and prompts us to become more and more like Jesus every day.

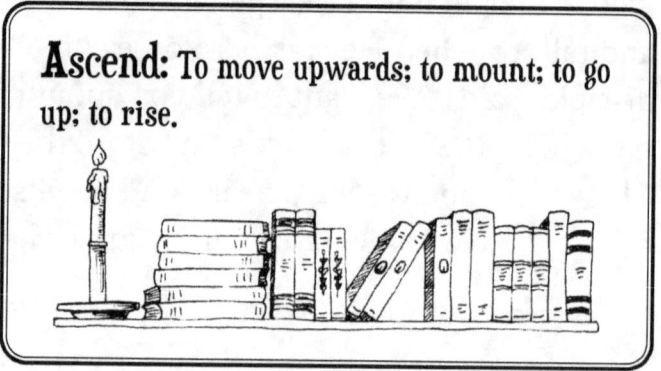

Ascend: To move upwards; to mount; to go up; to rise.

> # The Spirit came to dwell in the hearts of believers so we never have to be without God's presence.

After Jesus died, resurrected, and rose up (or *ascended*) to heaven, God the Father sent the Holy Spirit to be with us in a special new way. The Spirit came to dwell in the hearts of believers so we never have to be without God's presence even though Jesus is no longer with us in bodily form. His Spirit is here with us and in us.

When John the Baptist was preaching in the desert and baptizing his followers

---

26 Genesis 1:2.

27 Luke 1:35.

by immersion in water, he spoke of Jesus and the Holy Spirit when he said, "I baptize you with water, but the one who is coming will baptize you with the Holy Spirit."[28]

The Holy Spirit of God within us guides us, teaches us, reminds us of Scripture, helps us, shows us when we do wrong, and comforts us. We cannot see Him, but we can see evidence of His presence in the changes that happen in our lives when we walk with Him daily. As we grow in Christ, we see that where we once were hateful, the Holy Spirit enables us to feel love for others. Where we once were impatient, He helps us to be patient and gentle. Where we once were out of control, He helps us exercise self-control. Where we were depressed, the Holy Spirit now gives us a deep joy of life. All these good qualities are the fruits that the Holy Spirit will grow in us. "But the fruit that the Spirit produces in a person's life is love, joy, peace, patience, kindness, goodness, faithfulness, gentleness, and self-control."[29]

What fruits of the Spirit would you like for the Holy Spirit to help you develop?

_____

_____

_____

_____

_____

[28] Mark 1:8.

[29] Galatians 5:22–23.

Jesus called the Holy Spirit the Comforter: "And I will pray the Father, and He shall give you another Comforter, that He may abide with you for ever."[30]

The Holy Spirit is sometimes called the Helper. Jesus said, "When I go away I will send the Helper to you."[31] The Helper always points us to Jesus. Jesus says, "The Helper is the Spirit of truth who comes from the Father. When He comes, He will tell about Me."[32]

Seeing the Trinity in the Bible

We can see the Trinity in many ways in the Bible even though the word *trinity* does not appear in the Bible. For example, at the creation on the very first page, we see God the Father "created the sky and the earth." We see the Spirit of God "moved over the water." And finally, we see that God spoke the word: "Then God *said*, 'Let there be light!' And light began to shine."[33] As we learned, the Word is another name for Jesus, and everything was created through the Word that God speaks ("Then God said …"). So, we see the Trinity here at creation in the Father who spoke, the Spirit who moved, and the Word (Jesus) who let the light shine!

We can also see the Trinity in the way that God refers to Himself in the plural more than once in the Bible: "Now let's make humans who will be like Us."[34] He doesn't say "like Me" but instead speaks as though He is in a conversation. This shows the persons of the Trinity talking with one another.

When John the Baptist baptized Jesus, as soon as Jesus came up out of the water, "the sky opened, and he [John] saw God's Spirit coming down on Him [Jesus] like a dove. A voice from heaven said, 'This is My Son, the one

---

[30] John 14:16, KJV.

[31] John 16:7.

[32] John 15:26.

[33] Genesis 1:1–3.

[34] Genesis 1:26.

I love. I am very pleased with Him.'"[35] Here we see all three persons are present: Jesus, the Son, was baptized; the Holy Spirit descended like a dove; the Father spoke from heaven and was pleased.

We hear Jesus say, "The Father and I are one."[36] Also, Jesus commands us to baptize our disciples "in the name of the Father and the Son and the Holy Spirit."[37] This helps us understand that all three persons of the Trinity are unified with one purpose.

> # The Trinity shows the presence of love. Because God is three in one, love is given and received within the Godhead.

The Trinity shows the presence of love. Because God is three in one, love is given and received within the Godhead. Love is at the heart of God's being. It is that love that motivates the Father to send Jesus ("God loved the world so much …"), and He expects us to show that love to one another as a reflection of His nature. "God is love. Everyone who lives in love lives in God, and God lives in them."[38] The Trinity is the picture of perfect love.

---

[35] Matthew 3:16–17.

[36] John 10:30.

[37] Matthew 28:19.

[38] 1 John 4:16.

When we come to realize the truly awesome nature of God, we will naturally want to approach Him with the proper reverence and what is called the "fear of the Lord." This is not fear like the fear of spiders or the fear of darkness. It is fear based on the humbling understanding of how mighty God is and how small we are. "Let the whole world fear the LORD, and let everyone stand in awe of Him."[39]

The Trinity is difficult to understand. Some compare it to H2O (water), which has three forms: steam, water, and ice. Can you think of another example of three in one that is found in nature?

_____

_____

_____

_____

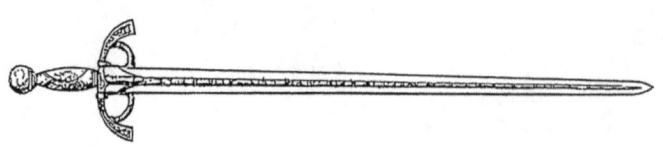

---

[39] Psalm 33:8, NLT.

HOW DO WE KNOW JESUS IS TRULY GOD?

Some people believe Jesus was a good teacher or prophet but not God. But what does the Bible say? While Jesus never used the exact words, "I am God," He claimed to be God in other words and ways. We know that the people of His time understood His claim to be God because of the way they reacted to Him. Some heard Him and right away wanted to condemn and kill Him. They falsely accused Him of blasphemy, which is a word for insulting God or claiming to be God. In the Bible, blasphemy is punishable by death. Jesus is the only person in history who can claim to be God *without* committing blasphemy! "Then the high priest tore his clothing to show his horror and said, 'Blasphemy! Why do we need other witnesses? You have all heard His blasphemy.'"[40]

> # God's name comes from the verb "to be," and it means that God is the very definition and essence of *being.*

One example of Jesus claiming to be God is when He refers to Himself as "I Am." This is the holy name of God by which He identifies Himself to Moses at the burning bush in the Old Testament. "I Am Who I Am."[41] This

---

[40] Matthew 26:65, NLT.

[41] Exodus 3:14.

name comes from the verb "to be," and it means that God is the very definition and essence of *being*. Jesus said, "I AM the good shepherd."[42] "I AM the light of the world."[43] "I AM the bread that gives life,"[44] and other such I AM statements. When people asked Jesus who He thought He was, He replied, "The fact is, before Abraham was born, I AM."[45] The people got so angry at this that they picked up stones to throw at Him. This is because they knew He was speaking of Himself as God, and they saw it as blasphemy.

When Jesus publicly forgave sins, He was doing something that only God could do. Some asked the question, "Why does this man say things like that? What an insult to God! No one but God can forgive sins."[46] The disciples and apostles knew Jesus was God. Paul referred to "our great God and Savior Jesus Christ."[47] The disciple Thomas addressed Jesus as "my Lord and my God!"[48]

Jesus did other things that only God could do. He gave sight to the blind, made the lame walk, opened the ears of the deaf, and brought dead people back to life. All these miracles were foretold in the Old Testament, and it was understood that only God could perform them. The people around Jesus who saw Him do these things remembered the Old Testament promises: "Look, your God will come and punish your enemies. He will come and give you your reward. He will save you. Then the eyes of the blind will be opened so that they can see, and the ears of the deaf will be opened so that they can

---

42 John 10:11, 14.

43 John 9:5.

44 John 6:35, 48.

45 John 8:58.

46 Mark 2:7.

47 Titus 2:13.

48 John 20:28.

hear. Crippled people will dance like deer, and those who cannot speak now will use their voices to sing happy songs."[49]

The apostle Paul understood that Jesus is God. One way he showed this was by quoting an Old Testament prophet named Joel, who lived long before Jesus. Joel said, "Whoever calls on the name of the LORD shall be saved."[50] By speaking of "the LORD," Joel was referring to God. Paul quoted Joel, again saying, "Whoever calls on the name of the Lord shall be saved."[51] But when Paul said those words, he was referring to Jesus, because he knew that Jesus is God.

So, it is clear that the people of Jesus's day—even His enemies—understood that He claimed to be God. His disciples—the people who were with Him the most—understood that He was God. And the fact that He performed miracles proved that He was God. The greatest of all the miracles that showed Jesus was God was His resurrection from the dead.

Read John 20:26-29. Find in this passage where Jesus has a blessing just for you.

---

[49] Isaiah 35:4–6.

[50] Joel 2:32, NKJV.

[51] Romans 10:13.

41

WHAT IS THE RESURRECTION?

Jesus died on the cross and was laid in a tomb. He was there for three days and nights. On the morning of the third day, some women who were followers of Jesus came to the tomb to anoint His body, as was the custom in those days. To their surprise, they found that something miraculous had happened. The stone that covered the tomb was rolled away, and the tomb was empty. Jesus had risen from the dead! The women ran to tell the other disciples about what had happened. Little did they know that this event would change the world.

Then, Jesus appeared alive to over five hundred people. He invited the disciple Thomas to touch the wounds from His crucifixion. "Look at My hands and My feet. It's really Me. Touch Me. You can see that I have a living body; a ghost does not have a body like this."[52]

Jesus walked and ate with His disciples, and He taught them many things, including how His death and resurrection fulfilled the Old Testament prophecies. Before His death, He told His followers that He must be killed. "Then, on the third day, He would be raised from death."[53] The resurrection fulfilled not only Jesus's own words to His disciples but Old Testament prophecies from hundreds of years before that said the Christ had to die for the sins of the world and then live again. For example, the Old Testament prophet Isaiah said, "But the LORD was pleased with this humble servant who suffered such pain. Even after giving Himself as an offering for sin, He will see His descendants and enjoy a long life. He will succeed in doing what the LORD wanted."[54]

When Jesus was taken into custody to be crucified, His disciples became afraid and confused and deserted Him. Peter even denied knowing Jesus. But after Jesus's resurrection, they were unshakable in their faith and ready to tell the world that Jesus is Lord. They all went to their deaths boldly proclaiming

---

[52] Luke 24:39.

[53] Matthew 16:21.

[54] Isaiah 53:10.

the lordship of Jesus Christ. In his very first sermon, the apostle Peter declared, "Jesus is the one God raised from death. We are all witnesses of this. We saw Him." [55]

Read 1 Corinthians 15:3-8. What did you learn here about the people that Jesus appeared to after His resurrection? Name three of these people.

_____

_____

_____

The Most Important Event

The resurrection of Jesus Christ is the most important event in human history. It is also the essential belief for the Christian. All our faith in Jesus hangs on this singular event. Without the resurrection, Christianity has no meaning. Paul says, "If Christ has never been raised, then the message we tell is worth nothing. And your faith is worth nothing." [56]

The resurrection is proof that Jesus's sacrifice as "the Lamb of God who takes away the sin of the world" [57] was acceptable to God. That means our salvation and the promise of our eternal life because of His victory over death are secured. Because He lives, we also can live. "And this is the promise that He has promised us— eternal life." [58] Jesus says, "I AM the resurrection and

[55] Acts 2:32.

[56] 1 Corinthians 15:14.

[57] John 1:29, NKJV.

[58] 1 John 2:25, NKJV.

the life. He who believes in Me, though he may die, he shall live. And whoever lives and believes in Me shall never die. Do you believe this?"[59]

Look at that last question Jesus asks above. *"Do you believe this?"* Here, Jesus asks the most important question of all—the question everyone must answer. It is a matter of life and death. When faced with this question, not answering is the same as saying no. The resurrection of Jesus gives a powerful and persuasive invitation

> Jesus's question, "Do you believe this?" is the question everyone must answer.

for us to believe in Jesus Christ. Let your faith in the resurrection and the hope of glory that comes from it shine as a beacon through your testimony. "God will also count us as righteous if we believe in Him, the one who raised Jesus our Lord from the dead. He was handed over to die because of our sins, and He was raised to life to make us right with God."[60]

In honor of this wondrous event and the joy that it means for us, Christians celebrate Easter, or Resurrection Sunday, every year.

How does learning about the resurrection change your understanding of what the Easter holiday is all about?

_____

_____

_____

_____

[59] John 11:25–26, NKJV.

[60] Romans 4:24–25, NLT.

WHAT IS THE BIBLE?

The Bible is a large book that is a collection of many smaller books, such as the book of Genesis (the first book of the Bible) and the book of Revelation (the last book of the Bible). It contains many types of writing, including history, prophecy, poetry, eyewitness testimony, and prayer.

The books of the Bible were written by dozens of writers over the course of thousands of years. Together, they carry a single message—the message of God's love for His people and His plan of redemption through His Son, Jesus.

How can it be that so many writers over such a long period tell one story? It is because God breathed His Spirit into all the human authors and caused His message to come through them. In the Bible, we have a direct line from God to us. The Holy Spirit inspired the authors to write it. And the Holy Spirit gives us a hunger to read it and the ability to understand it.

> **The Holy Spirit inspired the authors to write it. And the Holy Spirit gives us a hunger to read it and the ability to understand it.**

And even though it was written so long ago, the Bible is still current. It helps us make sense of our modern world. It teaches us about the character and nature of God. It strengthens our faith. It is our spiritual food.

45

Memorization: The devil once tried to tempt Jesus to obey him when Jesus was weak from fasting for a very long time. He commanded Jesus to turn stones into bread so He could eat. Jesus's answer to the devil is found in Matthew 4:4. It teaches us that Jesus considers the Word of God that we have in our Bibles to be more important food than bread. Memorize this Scripture in any version you prefer. You can use this version:

"But Jesus told him, 'No! The Scriptures say, "People do not live by bread alone, but by every word that comes from the mouth of God."'" [61]

Some people have Bibles that have been passed down to them from their fathers or mothers. Some have been given a Bible as a very special gift from a dear friend or church. We may cherish our Bibles. But even though they may be precious to us, the physical books themselves are not as important as what is written in them. The power of the Word of God is not in the book—the book is not a magical object. The power is in the mighty words of God that are in the book—whether those words are written, recited from memory, or read from a book, computer, or mobile phone Bible app.

Inspiration

God is the Master Author who inspired the human writers of the Bible. The word *inspired* means God-breathed, and we read that "all Scripture is inspired by God and is useful to teach us what is true and to make us realize what is wrong in our lives. It

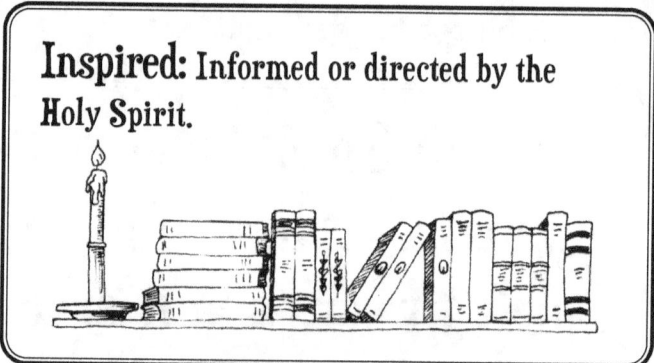

Inspired: Informed or directed by the Holy Spirit.

corrects us when we are wrong and teaches us to do what is right. God uses it to prepare and equip His people to do every good work." [62]

---

[61] Matthew 4:4, NLT.

[62] 2 Timothy 3:16–17, NLT.

Simply put, the entire Bible is the Word of God, and it is the final authority for what we Christians believe and how we are to live.

The Bible is not presented like a textbook, with point-by-point explanations to move an argument forward in a straight line. Instead, Christians study the Bible as a whole, looking at how God reveals Himself in many ways and how the different parts of the Bible refer to each other and all point to Jesus.

For example, we learn a lot about Jesus when we notice how He Himself quoted the Old Testament (He and the New Testament authors called the Old Testament "Scripture"). Once, Jesus went into a local synagogue, or religious assembly, and read aloud from the prophet Isaiah, where Isaiah speaks of one to come who is anointed to release captives and free the oppressed.[63] After reading this aloud, Jesus went on to say, "While you heard Me reading these words just now, they were coming true!"[64] In other words, Jesus was making the connection between Isaiah's words in the Old Testament, written seven hundred years before Jesus lived, and His mission that we read about in the New Testament. He was saying that He was the fulfillment of that Old Testament prophecy!

The Old Testament

The Bible is divided into two main parts: the Old Testament and the New Testament. The Old Testament was written mostly in the Hebrew language, and it focuses on

---

[63] Read about this in Luke 4:14–21.

[64] Luke 4:21.

> **God chooses the most lowly and unlikely people to do His will. By choosing the weakest, He shows His strength.**

the history of one particular people that God chose to be His priests. They were to be a light to the nations,[65] as God wanted to bless the whole world through them. This group of people was named after one of its early fathers—Jacob, whom God renamed Israel. So, this people is known in the Bible as Israel, Israelites, Jacob, Judah (after one of Jacob's sons), Hebrews, or Jews.

This people was not special in any way. They did not have anything that would make God want them in particular—in fact they were the smallest nation. They are an example of how God chooses the most lowly and unlikely people to do His will. By choosing the weakest, He shows His strength.

God made a promise to Abraham, a Hebrew, and kept that promise throughout history. "Why did the LORD love and choose you [Israel]? It was not because you are such a large nation. You had the fewest of all people! ... The LORD did this because He loves you and He wanted to keep the promise He made to your ancestors [Abraham, Abraham's son Isaac, and Isaac's son Jacob/Israel]."[66] God planned to include everyone in the whole world in His original promise of blessing, and He fulfilled His promise through the shed blood of His Son, Jesus, who was a descendant of Abraham, Isaac, and Jacob, "and from their race, according to the flesh, is the Christ."[67]

Sadly, the history of God's relationship with Israel as a people is not always a pretty picture. They were many times disobedient and self-willed, just like

---

65 Isaiah 60:3.

66 Deuteronomy 7:7–8.

67 Romans 9:5, ESV.

Adam and Eve and you and me. They rejected God over and over again. God chastised them, just as we do our children, but also extended mercy to them because He never stopped loving them, just as we love our children. They returned to Him in repentance over and over again, only to forget Him yet again.

Still, God never broke His promise to Israel and always remained faithful even when they were unfaithful. He promised them, "The descendants of Israel will never stop being a nation. That would happen only if I lost control of the sun, moon, stars, and sea." [68] "The LORD will not reject His people; He will not abandon His special possession." [69] And this is repeated in the New Testament: "No, God has not rejected His own people, whom He chose from the very beginning." [70]

The people of Israel are a mirror for us to see our own struggles as we try to live the Christian life. We can learn from Israel's victories and failures. But mostly, we learn about God. We can be encouraged by the faithfulness of God toward

> **Remember, just as the Lord loved and never gave up on Israel, He loves you and never gives up on you.**

---

[68] Jeremiah 31:36.

[69] Psalm 94:14, NLT.

[70] Romans 11:2, NLT.

Israel despite their failures. Remember, just as the Lord loved and never gave up on Israel, He loves you and never gives up on you. Your failures are only a temporary setback—they don't define you. "If we are not faithful, He will still be faithful, because He cannot be false to Himself." [71]

If God were to break His promises to Abraham, what would that say about His promises to you? How would that affect your faith in Him?

_____

_____

_____

_____

The New Testament

Now we'll talk about the New Testament. While the Old Testament speaks of Jesus in prophecy and teaching pictures, the New Testament introduces Jesus as a man who came to live among people on earth. The New Testament begins with the details of Jesus's birth, which took place hundreds of years after the events recorded in the Old Testament. Jesus's life as recorded in the New Testament gives the proof of His messiahship. (The word *messiah* means "Christ," or "anointed one.")

Anointed: Set apart; consecrated with oil.

The New Testament was written in the Greek language, and it records Jesus's teachings and eyewitness accounts of His birth, life, ministry, death, and resurrection. It also records what happened to Jesus's closest followers after He left the earth to return to His Father in heaven. It contains letters and teachings by His disciples and apostles and ends with prophecies about the return of Jesus.

---

[71] 2 Timothy 2:13.

The prophecies point to a time in the future that is the grand finale of God's great plan to dwell with humanity, with King Jesus reigning on His throne forever.

In the New Testament, we see a completion of God's promise to Abraham when He said, "I will use you [Abraham] to bless *all the people on earth*."[72] In other words, the blessing of salvation God has for humanity is for the Jews and for the rest of the world (known as Gentiles) as well. "His purpose was to make the two groups [Jews and Gentiles] become one in Him. By doing this He would make peace. Through the cross Christ ended the hate between the two groups. And after they became one body, He wanted to bring them both back to God. He did this with His death on the cross."[73] Gentiles are now included in the blessing of Abraham. The Bible calls the Jews and Gentiles who come together to worship Him "one new people."[74] Jews and Gentiles who follow Jesus together form the priesthood of all believers. "You are royal priests, a holy nation, God's very own possession. As a result, you can show others the goodness of God, for He called you out of the darkness into His wonderful light."[75]

> # Some call the Bible a love letter to humanity.

[72] Genesis 12:3.

[73] Ephesians 2:15–16.

[74] Ephesians 2:15, NLT.

[75] 1 Peter 2:9, NLT.

A Love Letter

Taken together, the Bible—Old and New Testament together—is the treasured Word of God. Some call it a love letter to humanity. It is worthy of a lifetime of study, and we can never reach the end of all its meaning. "The rain and snow come down from the heavens and stay on the ground to water the earth. They cause the grain to grow, producing seed for the farmer and bread for the hungry. It is the same with My Word. I send it out, and it always produces fruit. It will accomplish all I want it to, and it will prosper everywhere I send it." [76]

We talked about the Bible as a living book. The Holy Spirit helps us understand it, and without the Spirit of God, we cannot accept or understand the spiritual truths that are in the Bible. "People who do not have God's Spirit do not accept the things that come from His Spirit. They think these things are foolish. They cannot understand them, because they can only be understood with the Spirit's help." [77] When you pray, ask the Holy Spirit to give you understanding as you read your Bible. You can also get help in understanding your Bible from mature Christian teachers in your church or community.

How often do you eat food? What would happen if you did not eat for a day? For a few days? For a week? What about your spiritual food found in the Bible—what might happen if you don't eat your spiritual food—that is, read the Bible—for a week? What do you think that says about how often you should read your Bible?

_____

_____

_____

_____

_____

[76] Isaiah 55:10–11, NLT.

[77] 1 Corinthians 2:14.

WHAT IS THE CHURCH?

As a believing Christian, you are now a member of what is called God's church. The word *church* here does not mean a building where religious services are held, and it does not refer to any one congregation or denomination (such as Lutheran, Baptist, Catholic, or Church of Christ). The "church of God" is spiritual. It is made up of all the people who now believe, will believe, or ever have believed in Jesus Christ as their Savior.

Church: The collective body of Christians, or of those who profess to believe in Christ, and acknowledge Him to be the Savior of mankind.

The Body

The Bible paints a picture of the church as a body with Jesus as the head. "He is the head of the body, which is the church." [78] Each Christian is a part of that body and adds to it, each in our own way. Just as hands, feet, eyes, and mouths each have different roles to play in a physical body, each member of the "body of Christ" plays a different role. All members are necessary to the body as a whole, and no member is unimportant.

[78] Colossians 1:18.

> ## God has given each believer a unique and special gift to bring to the church.

One member of the body of Christ might have the gift of healing and pray for the sick. Another might be a gifted teacher. Yet another might be especially generous in giving. Still another might be a wonderful encourager. God has given each believer a unique and special gift to bring to the church, and the Holy Spirit helps you recognize and use your gift for the benefit of all the members of His church. What is the purpose of your special gift? You are to build up the church with your gifts. "Christ gave these gifts to prepare God's holy people for the work of serving, to make the body of Christ stronger."[79]

You can ask the Holy Spirit to show you what special gift you have to offer the church. Also, your gifts might change over time. You may receive a special new gift for the needs of a particular moment. The Holy Spirit knows what gifts are best for you at any given time.

"There are different kinds of spiritual gifts, but they are all from the same Spirit. There are different ways to serve, but we serve the same Lord. And there are different ways that God works in people, but it is the same God who works in all of us to do everything."[80]

Read 1 Corinthians 12:4-11 and Romans 12:4-8 to get an idea of some of God's gifts. Then pray to God that the Holy Spirit would show you the special gift He has for you at this time.

_____

_____

_____

_____

_____

[79] Ephesians 4:12.

[80] 1 Corinthians 12:4–6.

The Bible also paints a picture of Jesus's church as His bride, with Jesus as the Bridegroom. "Christ died so that He could give the church to Himself like a bride in all her beauty. He died so that the church could be holy and without fault, with no evil or sin or any other thing wrong in it."[81]

Unity of the Body

Just as all the parts of the physical body work together, everyone in God's church body works together to fulfill the purpose of the church, which is to glorify God, love and serve one another, and deliver the good news of Jesus to the world. We are unified as a family by our shared belief in Jesus, and we can call each other brothers and sisters in Christ. We are all different, but we are all one body. God wants the members of His church to love each other. "All people will know that you are My followers if you love each other."[82]

As a body, we are to be responsible and accountable to one another. This helps us stay on the spiritual warrior's path and get back on the path when we fall. When we come together to worship, we are blessed and encouraged by one another. We have the joy of being part of a wonderful family worshiping God together. We learn to love those members of the body that we find difficult to love, knowing that this is also part of our spiritual growth. Jesus prayed, "Father, I pray that all who believe in Me can be one."[83]

---

[81] Ephesians 5:27.

[82] John 13:35.

[83] John 17:21.

As a body, we can go deeper in our spiritual growth by studying the Word together. Those who are older in their Christian walk are able to teach the younger. "We should think about each other to see how we can encourage each other to show love and do good works. We must not quit meeting together, as some are doing. No, we need to keep on encouraging each other."[84]

You may be confused about all the denominations of churches you see in your communities. They vary in some ways—such as, they may conduct their services differently. They may be more or less excited in their style of worship. Some may hold to older traditions and styles while others are more modern. You might find different music played or sung, or the way people dress might be different. The church buildings may be grand or humble.

But God's church includes all believing Christians who faithfully follow the teachings of the Bible, regardless of denomination. Within God's church, our shared faith is more important than our differences, and in heaven there will be no denominations. We will all worship as one—the singular church of God. We are all Jesus's one true bride.

Why do you think Jesus cares so much about unity in the church, or the body, of Christ?

_____

_____

_____

_____

_____

[84] Hebrews 10:24–25.

WHAT IS WATER BAPTISM?

Washing in water was an ancient Jewish custom for ritual purification in the Old Testament days. God said, "I will sprinkle pure water on you and make you pure. I will wash away all your filth."[85] In the New Testament, we read about John the Baptist. That name, "the Baptist," simply means that John was one who baptized others by submerging them in water. John called people out to a spot in the wilderness to repent of their sins and be baptized as a spiritual purification and a physical sign of their repentance.

John played a very important role in the ministry of Jesus. When John was born, "Zechariah, John's father, was filled with the Holy Spirit and told the people a message from God,"[86] saying that John would grow up to be the one to announce the coming of the Messiah, or Christ, Jesus. About John, the Holy Spirit, speaking through Zechariah, said, "Now you, little boy, will be called a prophet of the Most High God. You will go first before the Lord to prepare the way for Him. You will make His people understand that they will be saved by having their sins forgiven."[87]

This was a fulfillment of an Old Testament prophecy that spoke of one who was to come to announce the coming of the Christ. In the Old Testament, that person was named Elijah. Jesus Himself identified John

---

[85] Ezekiel 36:25.

[86] Luke 1:67.

[87] Luke 1:76–77.

the Baptist as the one who came in the spirit of Elijah: He said, "John is Elijah. He is the one they said would come."[88]

John the Baptist came "preaching that people should be baptized to show that they had repented of their sins and turned to God to be forgiven,"[89] saying, "Repent of your sins and turn to God, for the Kingdom of Heaven is near."[90] His message was exactly the same as the message Jesus brought when He began His ministry: "Repent of your sins and turn to God, for the Kingdom of Heaven is near."[91]

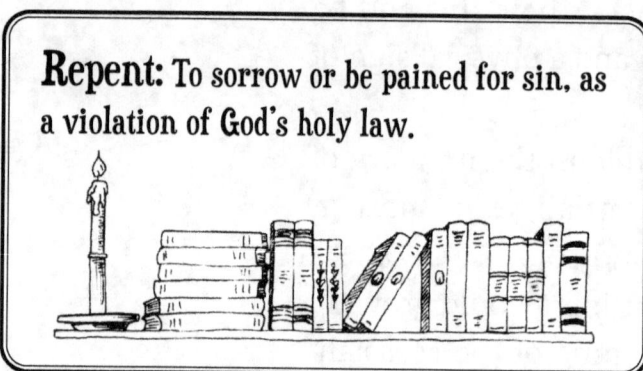

Repent: To sorrow or be pained for sin, as a violation of God's holy law.

Jesus went out to the wilderness to John the Baptist so He could be baptized by him. When Jesus came to John, John recognized who Jesus was—that He was the Messiah, or Christ—and proclaimed, "Look, the Lamb of God. He takes away the sins of the world!"[92]

John did not feel worthy to baptize Jesus, but Jesus insisted. "After His baptism, as Jesus came up out of the water, the heavens were opened and he [John] saw the Spirit of God descending like a dove and settling on Him [Jesus]. And a voice from heaven said, 'This is My dearly loved Son, who brings Me great joy.'"[93]

Jesus spoke of the importance of baptism when He commanded His disciples to "go and make followers of all people in the world. Baptize them in the

---

[88] Matthew 11:14.

[89] Luke 3:3, NLT.

[90] Matthew 3:2, NLT.

[91] Matthew 4:17, NLT.

[92] John 1:29.

[93] Matthew 3:16–17, NLT.

> # And a voice from heaven said, "This is My dearly loved Son, who brings Me great joy."

name of the Father and the Son and the Holy Spirit."[94] It is clear from this that Jesus expected all His followers to be baptized. After Jesus died, rose, and ascended to the Father, His disciples began preaching the need to repent of sins and be baptized. In the apostle Peter's very first sermon, he declared, "Repent of your sins and turn to God, and be baptized in the name of Jesus Christ for the forgiveness of your sins."[95]

In the Bible, we read that an official from Ethiopia came to worship among the Jews. As he was studying his Bible, God sent a Jesus follower named Philip to teach him about Jesus. As soon as the Ethiopian understood, he believed. "While they were traveling down the road, they came to some water. The official said, 'Look, here is water! What is stopping me from being baptized?' Philip answered, 'If you believe with all your heart, you can.' The official said, 'I believe that Jesus Christ is the Son of God.' Then the official ordered the chariot to stop. Both Philip and the official went down into the water, and Philip baptized him."[96]

---

[94] Matthew 28:19.

[95] Acts 2:38, NLT.

[96] Acts 8:36–38.

In the Old Testament, God gave us a teaching picture of baptism when He brought a great flood of water upon the earth. This flood was intended to cleanse the earth of those people who had dirtied it with their unrepentant sinfulness. God gave us another teaching picture when He led the children of Israel through the parted waters of the Red Sea. He led them through waters from slavery to freedom—from a foreign land to their own promised land where they would find a new identity as a nation. So, you can see that God uses water to bring renewal and new life.

Baptism is for all Christians. We are to be baptized. In baptism, we are ceremonially dipped in water. As we go under the water, we identify with the death of Jesus. As we come up out of the water, we identify with the resurrection of Jesus and our own rebirth into new life. Jesus meets us here in this sacrament. "So when we were baptized, we were buried with Christ and took part in His death. And just as Christ was raised from death by the wonderful power of the Father, so we can now live a new life."[97]

There are two confessions of faith in Jesus Christ. The first is the confession we make with our mouths when we declare our belief in Jesus and His death and resurrection. Then, having professed our belief in Jesus, we are to be baptized. Baptism is another sort of confession of faith. It is a sacrament, or solemn religious act, that publicly shows our community we have decided to follow Jesus.

Have you been baptized? Have you accepted Jesus Christ, and are you a member of a church community? If you have not been baptized, tell your pastor that you are ready. If you are not a member of a church community yet, seek out a church and a community where you can be baptized.

---

[97] Romans 6:4.

WHAT IS THE LORD'S SUPPER?

Another sacrament, or solemn religious act, of the Christian faith is the sharing of bread and wine in what is called the Lord's Supper, the Lord's Table, the Eucharist, or Communion. Jesus's final meal with His disciples was the traditional Jewish Passover meal, celebrating God's deliverance of the Israelites from slavery in Egypt, when the blood of a spotless lamb protected the people from death. At this last meal before He was crucified, Jesus told His disciples that this sharing of bread and wine was the start of the new covenant that had been promised centuries before.

What is a covenant? A covenant is like a contract or an agreement. In the Bible, a covenant is sacred and solemn, a binding agreement or promise. God's covenants are between God and His people.

Covenant: A mutual consent or agreement of two or more persons . . . ; a contract.

A New Covenant

Six hundred years before Jesus's final meal, the prophet Jeremiah spoke of a new covenant that was to come. God's people disobeyed His rules that He had etched onto stone tablets and given to Moses to teach them how to live their lives as a people dedicated to God. God told Jeremiah that because the people had disobeyed, He would write *a new covenant*, and He would write it directly onto their hearts and minds.

> # God told Jeremiah that because the people had disobeyed, He would write *a new covenant* directly onto their hearts and minds.

"'The day is coming,' says the LORD, 'when I will make a *new covenant* with the people of Israel and Judah. This covenant will not be like the one I made with their ancestors .... I will put My instructions deep within them, and I will write them on their hearts. I will be their God, and they will be My people .... And I will forgive their wickedness, and I will never again remember their sins.'"[98]

Six hundred years after Jeremiah said those words, at Jesus's final meal with His disciples, Jesus told them, "'Take, eat; this is My body.' Then He took the cup, and gave thanks, and gave it to them, saying, 'Drink from it, all of you. For this is *My blood of the new covenant*, which is shed for many for the remission of sins.'"[99] Jesus was referring to Jeremiah's prophecy of a new covenant. This is how the new covenant began: with the bread and the wine, fulfilling the words of Jeremiah and the promise of a new way of relating to God that does not depend on our ability to follow rules but on Jesus's saving work.

Remembering and Hoping

Jesus taught the disciples to eat the bread and drink the wine "in remembrance of Me."[100] We reverently remember that His blood (the wine) was spilled and

---

[98] Jeremiah 31:31–34, NLT.

[99] Matthew 26:26–28, NKJV.

[100] Luke 22:19, NKJV.

His body (the bread) was broken on the cross. When we take Communion, we remember the sacrifice of Jesus, "the Lamb of God who takes away the sin of the world." **101** This is a special time to commune with Jesus. He gave us this precious sacrament, and He meets us here.

> # Through Communion, the Lord feeds us a sacred spiritual meal that reminds us of His promise of a sweet future with Him in His forever kingdom.

But Communion is not just about remembering. When the people of Israel wandered in the wilderness, God gave them a heavenly bread tasting of honey. With this bread, called *manna*, He kept them alive, taught them to depend on Him, and gave them hope for a future in the promised land—a land of milk and honey. In the same way, through Communion, the Lord gives us sacred spiritual bread that reminds us of His promise of a sweet future with Him in His forever kingdom. The Bible tells us that "every time you eat this bread and drink this cup, you are announcing the Lord's death *until He comes*

101 John 1:29, NLT.

again." [102] So, we take Communion in remembrance of what Jesus did in the past but also looking forward to His return, when we will be with Him in His presence forever. "I want you to know, I will not drink this wine again until that day when we are together in My Father's kingdom and the wine is new. Then I will drink it again with you." [103]

Have you experienced communion? If so, describe what it means to you. What thoughts go through your head when you are taking communion? What emotions do you feel? If you have not experienced communion, speak to your spiritual leader about how you can participate in this sacrament. Then write about what it meant to you and what you experienced when you took communion for the first time.

_____

_____

_____

_____

_____

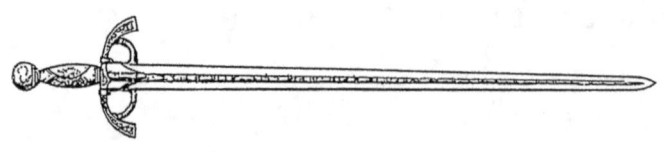

---

[102] 1 Corinthians 11:26, NLT.

[103] Matthew 26:29.

WHAT IS THE SABBATH?

The word *sabbath* means "rest." The Sabbath is a time to stop working and rest, and it began with God.

When God created the universe, He set up a pattern of six days of work followed by one day of rest. He wants us to follow this pattern. The fourth of the ten commandments is this: "You must remember to keep the Sabbath a special day. You may work six days a week to do your job. But the seventh day is a day of rest in honor of the LORD your God. So on that day no one should work …. That is because the LORD worked six days and made the sky, the earth, the sea, and everything in them. And on the seventh day, He rested. In this way, the LORD blessed the Sabbath—the day of rest. He made that a very special day."[104]

> # Instead of focusing on all the things *you do*, this one day a week is your chance to focus on what *God did.*

The Sabbath is a day to rest, recharge, and set your mind on things of God. Instead of focusing on all the things *you do*, this one day a week is your chance to focus on what *God did.* God did a work of salvation that made it possible for you to be restored and have life everlasting with Him. It was not your doing—it was all His doing. So, on the seventh day, you rest and remember His work.

---

[104] Exodus 20:8–11.

A Pattern of Sevens

The Bible repeats the Sabbath pattern in many ways. For example, Noah sends out a dove from the ark as the waters of the great flood are starting to go down, and he does so every seventh day. Also, God commanded Israel to let the land rest, or take a Sabbath, every seventh year. And every seven-times-seventh (that is, every forty-ninth) year, Israel was to hold a jubilee year when all debts were canceled. Seven is a number that God uses to represent completeness. As you read the Bible, you will see this number quite a bit.

The honoring of the Sabbath has practical importance. We need to balance our work life with times of rest. We need a day when we stop striving. When we work nonstop day after day, we get so wrapped up in our routine tasks that we don't make time to think about the things of God. This causes mental and physical exhaustion and causes our productivity and the quality of our work to go down. It is not natural.

Not only that, but the more we focus on the things we do, the less room there is in our thoughts for the things that God does and has already done for us. When we pause and take a day to rest, read the Bible, meet with other believers, pray, and think about God, we remember how dependent we are on His works. We remember that Jesus "sustains everything by the mighty power of His command."[105] We are rejuvenated, resting in Him. On the Sabbath, we can remember that God only asks us to do one sort of "work." "The people asked Jesus, 'What does God want us to do?' Jesus answered, 'The work God wants you to do is this: to believe in the one He sent.'"[106] "So let us do our best to enter that rest."[107]

> "The work God wants you to do is this: to believe in the one He sent."

---

[105] Hebrews 1:3, NLT.

[106] John 6:28–29.

[107] Hebrews 4:11, NLT.

When the nation Israel was wandering in the wilderness, God provided a special heavenly bread for them to gather from off the ground, prepare, and eat every day. It was called manna. In order to teach His people that they were to honor the Sabbath, God provided twice as much bread on the day before the Sabbath so they would not have to go out and gather it on the Sabbath. If they tried to gather more than they needed on any day other than the day before the Sabbath, the manna would go bad before they could eat it. But by His miraculous power, the extra Sabbath portion never went bad. Jesus told the people of His day that He is like the manna, except He is better because He offers eternal life. He said, "I am the bread that came down from heaven. Whoever eats this bread will live forever."[108]

What work can you do to deserve the amazing love of God?

Lord of the Sabbath

While we see the importance of following the ancient commandment to observe the Sabbath, the Old Testament rules have a new meaning now. Jesus gave us a new understanding of the Sabbath, and *it is all about Him.* Let's remember that God is the one who created times and seasons. On the fourth day of the creation week, "God said, 'Let lights appear in the sky to separate the day from the night. Let them be signs to mark the seasons, days, and years.'"[109] He promised that "as long as the earth

[108] John 6:58.

[109] Genesis 1:14, NLT.

continues, there will always be a time for planting and a time for harvest. There will always be cold and hot, summer and winter, day and night on earth." [110] So you see, God is the Lord of the Sabbath.

One Sabbath day while Jesus and His disciples were passing through grainfields, the disciples began to pick the heads of grain and eat them. Some religious leaders scolded them for doing this on the Sabbath, claiming that doing so broke God's law. Jesus answered them by saying, "The Sabbath day was made to help people. People were not made to be ruled by the Sabbath." [111] What Jesus said next changed everything in our understanding of the Sabbath: "So the Son of Man is Lord, even over the Sabbath." [112] When Jesus spoke of the Son of Man, He was referring to Himself as God. He was saying that the Sabbath is a way of understanding Him as our true rest.

How can we understand and experience every day of the week as a Sabbath in Jesus?

_____

_____

_____

The point is that if you blindly follow the law of the Sabbath for the sake of following rules, you miss out on the true rest you receive in Jesus. He said, "Come to Me all of you who are tired from the heavy burden you have been forced to carry. I will give you rest." [113]

Many believe that after Jesus rose from the dead, the followers of Jesus changed their Sabbath day from Saturday to Sunday in recognition of this great event. "On Sunday we all met together to eat the Lord's Supper." [114] But the

---

[110] Genesis 8:22.

[111] Mark 2:27.

[112] Mark 2:28, NLT.

[113] Matthew 11:28.

[114] Acts 20:7.

Bible tells us not to get too focused on which day is the proper Sabbath for us. "Some think one day is more holy than another day, while others think every day is alike. You should each be fully convinced that whichever day you choose is acceptable." [115] Jesus's point is that *He is the Sabbath,* and that we honor the Sabbath by remembering Him. God is more concerned with your heart than with how well you follow all the strict rules.

> **God is more concerned with your heart than with how well you follow rules.**

The Sabbath rest can also be seen as a tithe of your time, similar to the way you give some of your earnings to the Lord. God has a special way of multiplying your giving when it seems that by giving you should have less. Giving God your time to rest in Him is an act of faith that He will make the best use of your time. He knows what is best for you and wants you to enjoy all the benefits of His cycle of work and rest. When you give up your work time to honor Him, you get more done when you are working. You can think of this as God math!

---

[115] Romans 14:5, NLT.

Fill in the columns under the two headings below. This gives you a chance to think about what you might do differently to honor God with your Sabbath.

How I Honor God with My Sabbath Now	How I Would Like to Honor God with My Sabbath

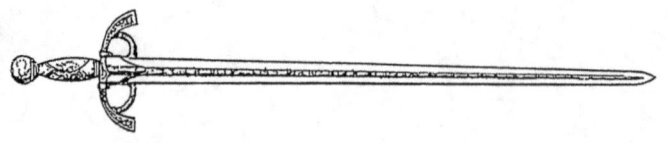

WHAT ARE PRAYING AND FASTING?

The Christian spiritual life is not complete without praying and fasting. Along with reading the Word of God every day, praying and fasting are basic practices that keep us spiritually nourished. They keep our minds firmly focused on God. Fasting should be done carefully and within limits, but there is no such thing as too much prayer. Paul says, "Pray without ceasing." [116]

Praying

Praying is how we communicate with God. We pray as a way to give Him adoration, worship, love, thanksgiving, and confession and to ask for the things we or others need. When we pray for others, that is called *intercession*. "Don't worry about anything, but pray and ask God for everything you need, always giving thanks for what you have." [117] We also pray in the hopes of hearing from God. The most common ways we hear from Him are through reading His Word and from inner promptings of the Holy Spirit within us.

The Bible tells us that God hears us when we pray. "Now this is the confidence that we have in Him, that if we ask anything according to His will, He hears us." [118]

> # We should pray that what we want is "according to His will."

[116] 1 Thessalonians 5:17, NASB.

[117] Philippians 4:6.

[118] 1 John 5:14, NKJV.

71

Our prayers should not be wish lists as though He were a genie who grants wishes. Instead, we should pray that what we want is "according to His will." Sometimes, the best way to pray is simply to say to Father God, as Jesus did when facing the terrible suffering of the cross, "Not My will, but Yours, be done."[119]

Jesus's disciples once asked Him, "Lord, teach us how to pray."[120] Jesus responded by teaching His disciples what is sometimes called the Lord's Prayer, or the Disciples' Prayer. You can find this model prayer in the Gospels of Matthew and Luke. Here is the Matthew version. Study this prayer line by line and think about its meaning. You can repeat this prayer yourself or use it as a starting point for your own words of prayer. Notice how Jesus teaches us to speak to the Father with highest honor, with the knowledge that we need Him for everything, and with the desire to align our will with the Father's will.

Our Father in heaven,
Hallowed be Your name.
Your kingdom come.
Your will be done
On earth as it is in heaven.
Give us this day our daily bread.
And forgive us our debts,
As we forgive our debtors.
And do not lead us into temptation,
But deliver us from the evil one.
For Yours is the kingdom and the power and the glory forever.
Amen.[121]

---

119 Luke 22:42, NKJV.

120 Luke 11:1.

121 Matthew 6:9–13, NKJV.

Memorize Matthew 6:9-13 and start each day with this prayer for one week. What do you notice after that time?

_____

_____

_____

_____

Jesus Himself was a beautiful example for us of a strong prayer life. He made sure to get away from the crowds and have private time in prayer with His Father. "Jesus went out to a mountain to pray. He stayed there all night praying to God. The next morning He called His followers. He chose twelve of them and called them apostles." [122] Notice that Jesus did not make that important decision about whom He would choose to be His apostles until He had spent a whole night in prayer.

> ## Jesus did not make that important decision until He had spent a whole night in prayer.

Like Jesus, you benefit from staying close to God in prayer before making important decisions in your life. But the ordinary, day-to-day moments can also be filled with prayer, as you thank God for your breakfast, praise Him for the sunshine, call on Him to help you finish your homework assignment, and ask Him to give you understanding of difficult passages of Scripture. Always have a

[122] Luke 6:12–13.

prayer on your lips—there is always a good reason to do so. "Because Your lovingkindness is better than life, my lips shall praise You. Thus I will bless You while I live; I will lift up my hands in Your name."[123]

Praying does not have to be done with folded hands and bowed head in a formal posture. You can pray anytime, anywhere, and in any position, speaking aloud or keeping silent. Sometimes, you don't even need words to pray. The Holy Spirit understands your groanings and can express your needs in language that God understands even if you can't form the right words. "We are very weak, but the Spirit helps us with our weakness. We don't know how to pray as we should, but the Spirit Himself speaks to God for us. He begs God for us, speaking to Him with feelings too deep for words. God already knows our deepest thoughts. And He understands what the Spirit is saying, because the Spirit speaks for His people in the way that agrees with what God wants."[124]

Sometimes, you might wish to use the words of the Bible as your prayer. You can find wonderful passages that say just what you are feeling. For example, you can pray Psalm 91:2 and make it your own: "I say to the LORD, 'You are my place of safety, my fortress. My God, I trust in you.'" In the 150 psalms, you will find every sort of emotion expressed—from fear to faith, from frustration to complete surrender to God, from joy to deep sorrow. Let the words of the psalmists and other Bible authors fill your heart and be on your lips. The example of the psalms shows that you can be totally truthful with God. Even if you are angry or have other negative feelings, do not be afraid to bring them to God in prayer.

Find a passage from the book of Psalms that you would like to use as your own prayer to God today.

You can take great comfort in knowing that even Jesus Himself is—right at this very moment—bringing your prayer needs before God. Isn't that amazing?

---

[123] Psalm 63:3–4, NKJV.

[124] Romans 8:26–27.

"He is sitting in the place of honor at God's right hand, pleading for us."[125] "He is able, once and forever, to save those who come to God through Him. He lives forever to intercede with God on their behalf."[126]

Faith vs. Feelings

> # How you are feeling has nothing to do with the truth of who God is.

During your times of prayer, you may or may not feel that God is listening. But how you are feeling has nothing to do with the truth of who God is. Your feelings can change from day to day and even moment to moment. At times, you may be overcome with feelings of gratitude, peace, love, excitement, or awe. Or you may feel abandoned, depressed, angry, or other negative feelings. You may feel God is very near, or you may feel He is very far away. But God is eternal and unchanging, regardless of how you feel. "Jesus Christ is the same yesterday, today, and forever."[127] How comforting to know that through all your ups and downs, there is One whose love for you never changes! You can depend on Him.

---

[125] Romans 8:34, NLT.

[126] Hebrews 7:25, NLT.

[127] Hebrews 13:8.

Have you ever felt during a time of prayer that God was very near to you? Have you ever felt during a time of prayer that He was very far from you? Read Psalm 139:7-10 and discuss.

_____

_____

_____

_____

Fasting

Our bodies need food every day. When we don't eat, our bellies cry out to be fed. When we fast, we deny that noisy hunger of the flesh by not eating for a period of time in order to take a different kind of nourishment: spiritual food—that is, the Word and presence of God. When we fast, we become very aware of how much our lives are guided by thoughts that begin with the words "I want." Paul speaks of desires like this: "For the desire of the flesh is against the Spirit, and the Spirit against the flesh; for these are in opposition to one another, in order to keep you from doing whatever you want."[128]

> When we fast, we become very aware of how much our lives are guided by thoughts that begin with the words "I want."

When you fast, God honors your willingness to sacrifice your comfort and the needs and desires of your body and mind. It is in the discomfort of your hunger pangs during fasting that you can be reminded to turn to God. You can also fast of other things besides food—for example, television, social media, sweets, junk food, or any other thing that takes up your attention. But it is the belly that most powerfully reminds you of the struggle between the flesh and the spirit.

[128] Galatians 5:17, NASB.

God allowed the ancient Israelites to hunger to remind them that He was their source of nourishment: "He humbled you and let you be hungry. Then He fed you with manna—something you did not know about before. It was something your ancestors had never seen. Why did the Lord do this? Because He wanted you to know that it is not just bread that keeps people alive. People's lives depend on what the LORD says."[129]

Fasting is never done without prayer. During your times of fasting, God may grant you new insight, or you may feel particularly close to God. You may become more aware of your need for God and His sustaining power in your life. Your understanding of your total dependence on Him will grow.

Sustain: To maintain; to keep alive; to support.

Jesus teaches that when you fast, you are not to brag about it or let others know, so that it does not become a cause for pride. "When you fast, don't make yourselves look sad like the hypocrites. They put a look of suffering on their faces so that people will see they are fasting. The truth is, that's all the reward they will get. So when you fast, wash your face and make yourself

---

[129] Deuteronomy 8:3.

look nice. Then no one will know you are fasting, except your Father, who is with you even in private. He can see what is done in private, and He will reward you."[130]

> # When you fast, wash your face and make yourself look nice. Then no one will know you are fasting, except your Father.

We read in Daniel 6 that Daniel's enemies conspired against him. They convinced the king, Darius, to sign a new law that anyone who prayed to any god except Darius would be thrown into the lion's den. They knew that Daniel prayed only to the one true God. When Daniel disobeyed the edict, they reported it to King Darius. Darius had no choice but to throw Daniel into the lion's den even though he loved Daniel and did not want to see him harmed. Read Daniel 6:18-28 to learn the rest of the story. Notice where fasting is mentioned and what happened. Discuss.

_____

_____

_____

_____

_____

---

[130] Matthew 6:16–18.

WHAT IS THE KINGDOM OF GOD?

After Jesus was baptized by John the Baptist, He began His ministry with these words: "Change your hearts and lives [or "repent"], because God's kingdom is now very near." [131] What did He mean by saying God's kingdom was near? He meant there is another kingdom, or realm, other than the worldly realm. In that other realm, there is a King who rules, and that King is different from earthly kings. He was referring to the kingship of God—the ultimate King—the Creator of the universe. By saying that God's kingdom is now very near, He was referring to Himself and His presence on earth—near to us—as He was beginning to spread His message of salvation. When He said, "Change your hearts," or "repent," He was inviting all people to turn from their sins, return to faith in the one true God, and become citizens in His *heavenly* kingdom.

> He was referring to Himself and His presence on earth—near to us—as He was beginning to spread His message of salvation.

The kingdom of God is sometimes called the kingdom of heaven. "God is spirit," and "the people who worship

---

[131] Matthew 4:17.

Him must worship in spirit and truth."[132] The heavenly kingdom is a spiritual kingdom, set apart from the kingdoms of this world.

Two Kingdoms

Christians live in two different worlds. One is the physical world, where we live for a time, working, playing, and meeting the challenges of daily life. It is a kingdom that we know will pass away one day. The other is the spiritual world, and because we are spiritual beings, we also live in this world. In the physical world, we enjoy God's creation and all the blessings He has for us. At the same time, we keep our attention on the spiritual world, remembering the spiritual battle we are in and looking to God for the power and wisdom of His Word. Jesus tells us, "Here on earth you will have many trials and sorrows. But take heart, because I have overcome the world."[133]

In the physical world, we are to be loyal citizens of the nations where we live. We are to work and be a help to our families and communities. But

> **We must learn to be aware of and navigate both worlds.**

we are also citizens in God's eternal spiritual kingdom. As followers of Jesus, we live *in the* world but not *of* the world, as Jesus puts it.[134] We must learn to be aware of and navigate both worlds. But the more important world is the one that lasts forever. Rather than making the rewards of the physical world our main goal, we are to "*seek first* the kingdom of God and His righteousness."[135]

When Jesus walked on this earth, He established His kingdom in part. So, Jesus's kingdom has come, as we see in our own transformed lives and

---

132 John 4:24.

133 John 16:33, NLT.

134 John 17:16.

135 Matthew 6:33, HOLMAN CHRISTIAN STANDARD BIBLE (HCSB).

hearts. But we live in a fallen world—imperfect, with sin all around us. Rest assured, Jesus will return one day, and His kingdom will be fully established on earth forever. "We are citizens of heaven, where the Lord Jesus Christ lives. And we are eagerly waiting for Him to return as our Savior." [136]

While we see rulers, kings, presidents, and prime ministers controlling the earth today, one day their rule will pass away. While we see sin throughout the world today, one day sin will also pass away. "The Lord Himself will come down from heaven with a loud command, with the voice of the archangel, and with the trumpet call of God. And the people who have died and were in Christ will rise first. After that we who are still alive at that time will be gathered up with those who have died. We will be taken up in the clouds and meet the Lord in the air. And we will be with the Lord forever." [137]

At that time, we will say, "The world has now become the Kingdom of our Lord and of His Christ, and He will reign forever and ever." [138]

Sometimes, you will find that the two kingdoms you live in—the physical world and the spiritual world—don't see eye to eye. The things of the spiritual world can seem foolish to those who do not have their eyes open to see spiritual things. Unless the Holy Spirit opens people's eyes, they will see the things of the world as wise and the things of God as foolish. "If you think you are wise

---

[136] Philippians 3:20, NLT.

[137] 1 Thessalonians 4:16–17.

[138] Revelation 11:15, NLT.

by this world's standards, you need to become a fool to be truly wise. For the wisdom of this world is foolishness to God."[139] Jesus teaches us that rather than seeking to be loved by the world, we should expect to be hated in the world as His ambassadors, because the world hates Him.

Read Matthew 6:25-34. Here is verse 33:

"But seek first the kingdom of God and His righteousness, and all these things will be added to you."

Discuss what you think Jesus means by saying that "all these things will be added to you" in the context of Matthew 6:25-34.

_____

_____

_____

_____

_____

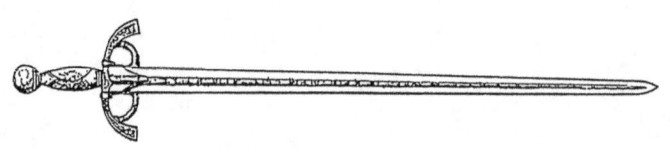

139 1 Corinthians 3:18–19, NLT.

WHO IS THE ENEMY OF GOD?

In the Great Battle between good and evil, we know very well who leads the charge on the side of the good—the One who loves you: the Victorious Warrior, Jesus. But who leads the charge on the evil side? Who is God's enemy? The answer is: the one who hates God, and because you are the object of God's love, he hates you. That one is the devil.

> # God's enemy first showed up in the Bible in the garden of Eden in the form of a snake.

God's enemy first showed up in the Bible in the garden of Eden in the form of a snake. His seductive lies led Adam and Eve to be puffed up in their pride. In that moment, they believed that somehow it was possible that they could be like God, as the snake claimed. And so, they willfully disobeyed God. This is when sin first came into the world and when people became part of the Great Battle of good against evil.

Jesus tells us that His enemy "was a murderer from the beginning.... Yes, the devil is a liar. He is the father of lies." "The thief's purpose is to steal and kill and destroy." He is the one "who leads the whole world into the wrong way." 140

The enemy has many names: Satan, the devil, the deceiver, the dragon, the snake, and the tempter, to name

---

140 John 8:44; John 10:10, NLT; Revelation 12:9.

just a few. His main purpose is to destroy the relationship between God and humanity. Why? Because "God created humans in His own image. He created them to be like Himself."[141] Because God has a special love for human beings, the enemy of God wants to destroy us and separate us from God. He will do anything to break our bond.

The Enemy and You

You may wonder what this has to do with you. While the Great Battle between God and His enemy takes place in the spiritual realm, you can see the effects of the devil's works all around you. Whenever you see broken lives, addiction, murder, chaos, and all the tragedies in the world, you are seeing his handiwork. Before you gave your life to Jesus, you "lived the way the world lives, following the ruler of the evil powers that are above the earth. That same spirit is now working in those who refuse to obey God."[142]

> Whenever you see broken lives, addiction, murder, chaos, and all the tragedies in the world, you are seeing the enemy's handiwork.

Now, because you are on God's side in the Great Battle, the enemy wants to bring his destruction to you. But don't let this scare you. God is infinitely more powerful than His enemy, and He has already defeated him. Jesus "defeated the rulers and powers of the spiritual world. With the cross He won the victory over them and led them away, as defeated and powerless prisoners for the whole world to see."[143]

---

141 Genesis 1:27.

142 Ephesians 2:2.

143 Colossians 2:15.

"We thank God who gives us the victory through our Lord Jesus Christ!" 144 In the end, the devil will be "thrown into the lake of fire and brimstone." 145 But until that time, we must recognize him because he is real. We must resist his temptations.

The Enemy Is a Loser

God's enemy has rulership over the world for a time. We don't know why God allows His enemy to have authority in the world. Yet, that rulership is only temporary and limited. Jesus assures us that "the ruler of this world will be thrown out." 146

How can you defeat the devil? Only by calling on Jesus can you defeat him. The Bible tells you to "humble your-selves before God. Resist the devil, and he will flee from you." 147 Let's review that two-part battle plan:

1. First, *humble yourself before God.* Submit to Him fully and confess He is the master of your life. If you need to confess any sin that has allowed the enemy to come into your life and make trouble, then do so in humility.

2. Second, *resist the devil.* Resist his temptations—his attempts to lure you into sin.

If you do these two things, the enemy has no choice but to flee—he has no power over you. "The one who is in you is greater than the one who is in the world." 148

144 1 Corinthians 15:57.

145 Revelation 20:10, NASB.

146 John 12:31.

147 James 4:7, NLT.

148 1 John 4:4.

Remember, you stand with the Victorious Warrior, Jesus, who has already defeated the evil one. You can rest in this assurance. In Jesus, you are victorious! Hold your head high! "In all these things we are more than conquerors through Him who loved us."[149]

Once, Jesus sent out His disciples to tell the surrounding towns that His kingdom had come. When they returned, the disciples were very excited that they had been able to do many things by the power of Jesus working in them, including casting the devil's demons out of people. Jesus responded by saying, "I have given you more power than he has."[150] But Jesus went on to say that the power to defeat demons was not as important as the fact that their names were written in the book of life. We learn here that although we can overcome the power of the devil by the power of Jesus, the better cause for rejoicing is that "your names are written in heaven."[151]

You can learn from Nehemiah, who had to deal with enemies that were trying to destroy his work of wall-building by throwing insults and lies at him and making false reports to the authorities. Nehemiah did not go out to meet with his enemies even though they tried hard to draw him into a fight. He simply focused on doing the right thing. He built his wall.[152] That is what you are to do as well when faced with the wiles of the enemy of God. Do not engage the enemy. Just do the next right thing.

> # Please know that not all bad things that happen to you are because of the devil.

---

[149] Romans 8:37, ESV.

[150] Luke 10:19.

[151] Luke 10:20.

[152] Read about it in Nehemiah 6.

Please know that not all bad things that happen to you are because of the devil. Sometimes, you are just in the wrong place at the wrong time, or you encounter people with bad intentions. And sometimes you make bad choices. "You are tempted by the evil things you want. Your own desire leads you away and traps you. Your desire grows inside you until it results in sin. Then the sin grows bigger and bigger and finally ends in death." [153] If you sin, you should expect that there will be consequences, even though you may have asked for and received the forgiveness of God.

When you realize that you have sinned, you should be quick to change your course—to repent. To repent means to change your heart, mind, and direction to turn away from sin and toward God. Instead of blaming the devil, look at the part you played. Confess, seek God's forgiveness, and get back on the right track. The more you allow for sinful habits, the more likely it is that the enemy will use your weakness to strengthen his position and influence you. Sin gives birth to more sin, and the more you allow for your sin, the more it will grow and spread. So, it is best to continually seek God's righteousness.

What are the two steps the Bible says will cause the devil to flee from you? Give an example of how that might look in your life.

_____

_____

_____

_____

_____

[153] James 1:14–15.

WHAT CHRISTIANITY IS NOT

As you begin to experience the wondrous spiritual blessings of God, do not make the mistake of thinking these blessings come from magic or that the work of God is magical. You should not think of Jesus as a magician, and Christianity does not work by magic. Nor is Jesus a djinn, jujuman, or genie to grant your wishes. He can't be accessed through a shaman or witch doctor. Jesus's power is not a toy for you to use for your own purposes.

> You should not think of Jesus as a magician, and Christianity does not work by magic. Nor is Jesus a djinn, jujuman, or genie to grant your wishes. He can't be accessed through a shaman or witch doctor. Jesus's power is not a toy for you to use for your own purposes.

Jesus won't magically make your troubles go away or your enemies suffer for hurting you. Amulets, love potions, spells, curses, talismans, crystals, shamanic incantations, palm reading, fortune telling, witch's brews, voodoo dolls, Ouija boards, and other occult practices and objects belong to the world of God's enemy, Satan. *None of that should be a part of your Christian life!*

At the very least, these things are a distraction to draw you away from the truth. At the worst, they give an opening for the enemy of God to enter your life and cause harm. This is called giving the enemy a *stronghold*, and he will use that stronghold to destroy you if he can. In that case, you must remove these behaviors and things from your life, renounce them, confess, and pray for deliverance. The name of Jesus has the power to free you from the enemy.

"The weapons we use in our fight are not the world's weapons but God's powerful weapons, which we use to destroy strongholds."[154]

The Christian walk is a holy spiritual pursuit. The power of Jesus is not found in objects or in magic spells. All you need to receive the best of what God has for you is found in following Jesus according to the Word of God.

One example of magical thinking among Christians is the misunderstanding of the Scripture where Jesus says, "If you ask for anything in My name, I will do it for you."[155] The magical thinking is that if you pray "in the name of Jesus," your wish will automatically be granted. Does this Scripture mean that Jesus will do anything you ask as long as you use the words "in Jesus's name"? "I want a new car, in the name of Jesus!" Or, "Make that person who hurt me fall off his roof, in Jesus's name!" What if you ask for something that is not in God's will? Will Jesus do it just because you used those words? Of

> **Jesus meant in this Scripture that when your heart is aligned with His heart and you ask for what is in harmony with His perfect judgment and will, He will do it.**

[154] 2 Corinthians 10:4, GOOD NEWS TRANSLATION (GNT).

[155] John 14:13.

course not! Jesus meant in this Scripture that when your heart is aligned with His heart and you ask for what is in harmony with His perfect judgment and will, He will do it.

When Jesus taught His disciples a model prayer, He included the line, "Your will be done,"[156] meaning you are to pray that God's will would be done. Rather than expecting Jesus to do *your* will by using His name as a magical chant, you are to align your spirit and desires with *His* perfect will.

Do you trust God enough with your problems to allow *His will* to be done in your life?

_____

_____

_____

_____

If you have a history of playing with magic, black magic, the occult, or Ouija boards; going to witch doctors, fortune tellers, palm readers, or seers; or engaging in any other unholy spiritual practices, now is the time to repent of those behaviors, remove all objects associated with those practices, and renounce those works of the enemy of God. Those practices are not of God. It is the will of God to free you from Satan's grip and embrace you as His precious child. He wants you to follow Him and leave behind the powers of darkness. "So humble yourselves before God. Resist the devil, and he will flee from you."[157] "The thief comes only to steal and kill and destroy. I came that they may have life and have it abundantly."[158]

---

[156] Matthew 6:10, NKJV.

[157] James 4:7, NLT.

[158] John 10:10, ESV.

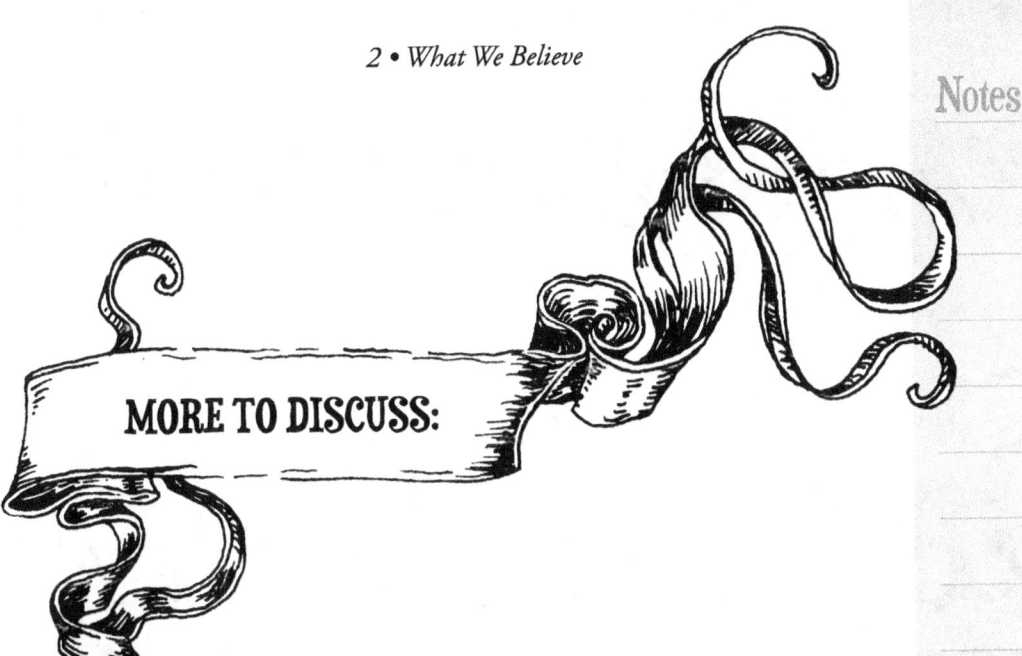

MORE TO DISCUSS:

3. What is the difference between the God of the Bible and other so-called gods?

4. Read Luke 11:1-45. How do you think witnessing Larazus coming forth from the tomb affected the disciples' understanding of who Jesus is?

5. We have come to the end of Part 2: "What We Believe." List three things you learned in Part 2 that you didn't know before. How does your new understanding strengthen your faith?

Day by Day

Christ is the one who gives me the strength I need to do whatever I must do.

Philippians 4:13

3 • Living the Christian Life

In Part 2, you learned some Christian basics—building blocks of the faith to give you a good foundation for your walk with Jesus. Now that you have this information, what do you do with it? How are you to live?

Our salvation in Messiah Jesus does not come from any works we do. But when we are saved, *we want* to do good works. "Faith by itself isn't enough. Unless it produces good deeds, it is dead and useless."[1] Faith and works go hand in hand. God has work for us to do. That work might be big or small in the world's eyes, but His eyes are the only ones that matter. Our work for today might be as small as saying a kind word. Or it might be a work that impacts many lives for the better.

> **"God made us to do good works, which God planned in advance for us to live our lives doing."**

[1] James 2:17, NLT.

Whatever it is, it is valuable in God's sight, and He has equipped us to do it. "In Christ Jesus, God made us to do good works, which God planned in advance for us to live our lives doing."[2]

Here in Part 3, you will learn how to apply the Christian basics as you live a life of *love, holiness, sharing the good news, worship, purity, stewardship,* and *study.* Let's start with first things first: a life of love.

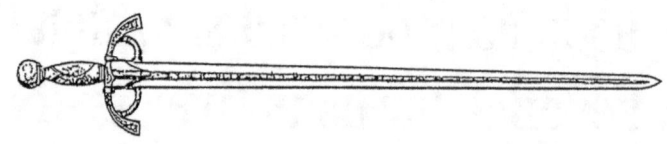

---

[2] Ephesians 2:10, NEW CENTURY VERSION (NCV).

A LIFE OF LOVE

"God is love; and he that dwelleth in love dwelleth in God, and God in him." God's kingdom shines with His love. You can best reflect His character by living a life of love. Jesus gave believers what is called the Great Commandment: "I give you a new command: Love each other. You must love each other just as I loved you. All people will know that you are My followers if you love each other."

Keep in mind how deeply and completely you are loved by God. This truth forms a foundation for your spiritual life because it explains God's purposes for you and all people. He made humans in His image. No other creature has this distinction. This quality of being made in God's image gives people their worth and applies to all equally. There is no human being on the face of the earth that is *not* made in God's image—even those who may seem unimportant in some people's eyes, like the elderly, the sick, the rejected and abandoned, the poor, those with mental or physical disabilities, the orphan, and the baby still in the womb.

When Jesus took the sin of humanity upon Himself, He did that for everyone. Every person you encounter is as much a beloved child of God, precious in His sight, as you are. You show your love for God by seeing others through His eyes and loving those He loves. "No one has ever seen God. But if we love each other, God lives in

---

3 1 John 4:16, KJV.

4 John 13:34–35.

us. If we love each other, God's love has reached its goal—it is made perfect in us."[5]

How have you experienced God's love in your life?

_____

_____

_____

_____

Serving Others

You can show your love for others by serving them, just as Jesus showed His love by serving the people He was with when He walked the earth. He loved them so much He even washed their feet like a lowly servant would do, out of His servant's heart. He did this to show His disciples how they should serve one another. "Whoever wants to be the most important must make others more important than themselves. They must serve everyone else."[6]

> Jesus loved them so much He even washed their feet like a lowly servant would do, out of His servant's heart. He did this to show His disciples how they should serve one another.

Our natural state is not to serve others but to serve ourselves and our own interests. We want all the good things and none of the bad. We want that last piece of chicken. When we do well, we want everyone to notice. When we

---

[5] 1 John 4:12.

[6] Mark 9:35.

behave badly, we want to avoid the consequences, and we justify ourselves with lots of good excuses. Basically, we want to do what we want to do—what benefits us most. That is the way we were before Christ.

But now, we are different. We have been born again from above and have the Holy Spirit of God working in us.

This doesn't mean you have to love everyone the way you love your mother, someone you know well and are deeply fond of, or someone you want to marry. Those are different kinds of love. Neighborly love means holding the concerns of others—even if those others are strangers or even enemies—as just as important as your own concerns.

What does the other person need? What is he going through? How can you help her overcome a challenge she faces? How can you be a help to this stranger or that foreigner? How can you show respect to this elder who is being disrespected or that widow without enough to eat? How can you show regard for that person no one likes to be around?

"We must not get tired of doing good. We will receive our *harvest of eternal life at the right time*. We must not give up. When we have the opportunity to do good to anyone, we should do it. But we should give special attention to those who are in the family of believers."[7]

How can you serve someone in need today? Go do it!

_____

_____

_____

[7] Galatians 6:9–10.

97

Sacrificial Love

Serving others will always involve a sacrifice on your part. Sitting by while you could be a help to another does not cost you anything. But once you step out to help another, it will cost you in either comfort, time, money, effort, attention, or having your way. Serving always has a cost.

But notice there is a promise given in the verse above. It says that you will receive a "harvest of eternal life at the right time" when you do good to anyone. And while you serve for the sake of being a help to others and not for a reward, you also can be comforted in knowing that any loss you suffer to be of service is temporary and tiny in comparison with your gains in the kingdom—that is, your eternal reward. But you also get an immediate reward, as the cost of sacrifice becomes a source of joy rather than a burden to bear. When you see how your sacrifice helps another and honors God, your giving becomes a beautiful expression of worship.

> Once you step out to help another, it will cost you. But you get an immediate reward, as the cost of sacrifice becomes a source of joy rather than a burden to bear.

Sometimes, loving your neighbor is hard to do. How do you do it? You can only do it when you develop the mind of Christ. "Let this mind be in you, which was also in Christ Jesus: who ... took upon Him the form of a servant."[8] Ask the Holy Spirit to give you the mind of Christ.

How would the world be different if everyone loved their neighbor?

_____

_____

_____

[8] Philippians 2:5–7, KJV.

The Good Samaritan

Jesus gives us an example of loving your neighbor as yourself. In His parable of the Good Samaritan, He tells of a man who was going on his way and was beat up by robbers. They took his clothes and left him for dead on the road. A priest came by and did not stop to help him. In fact, he crossed to the other side of the road so as not to get too close to him. Then another holy man came by and did the same.

But along came a Samaritan—a man of a different race. This Samaritan saw the man lying on the road and felt sorry for him. He cared for his wounds and gave him clothes to wear. He put him on his donkey and took him to a hotel. He paid the hotelkeeper and promised to pay more when he returned. "Take care of this hurt man," he told the hotelkeeper.

After telling this story, Jesus asked, "Which one of these three men do you think was really a neighbor to the man who was hurt by the robbers?" Was it the priest? The other holy man? Or the Samaritan?

The answer to Jesus's question is clear. The true neighbor was the man who cared for a stranger in need even though it meant a sacrifice of time, attention, money, and goods, and even though the one in need was different from him. Jesus asks us to "go and do the same." We are to show compassion for others, even those others

> # We are even to show compassion for those who are not like us.

Read the whole story at Luke 10:30–37.

who are not like us. This is how Jesus loves us, and it is how He wants us to love each other. When we love others, we are loving Him.

One example of loving others is forgiving. Jesus asked that the Father forgive the very people who crucified Him. If He could forgive them, then we should also be forgivers. This is part of how we love our neighbors as ourselves. Jesus described Himself as "gentle and humble in heart." [10] We should also be gentle and humble in the way we treat others. Our message of the good news of Jesus and His offer of salvation should be wrapped in gentleness, humility, and reverence. We should be slow to take offense and quick to make peace. These are all ways we show love.

"So prepare your minds for service." [11] You may wish to greet each morning with a prayer on your lips asking God to give you His love that you can then give to others. It is only with God's help that you can accomplish these difficult things. While it is easy to love the lovely people around you, it is hard to love the unlovely. This is where the love of Jesus can shine through you. "God has poured out His love to fill our hearts through the Holy Spirit He gave us." [12] This is part of what it means to have the mind of Christ.

Memorize 1 John 4:10-11 in any version. Here is one you can use:

"This is real love—not that we loved God, but that He loved us and sent His Son as a sacrifice to take away our sins. Dear friends, since God loved us that much, we surely ought to love each other." [13]

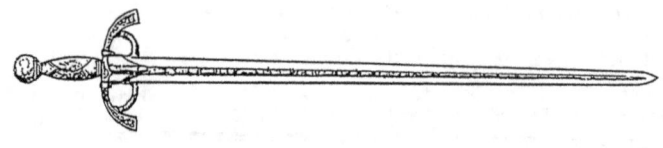

---

[10] Matthew 11:29, NASB.

[11] 1 Peter 1:13.

[12] Romans 5:5.

[13] 1 John 4:10–11, NLT.

A LIFE OF HOLINESS

Let's talk about what it means to be holy. "Jesus Christ did the things God wanted Him to do. And because of that, we are made holy through the sacrifice of Christ's body." Being holy is a gift from God that you receive at the moment of your salvation. It is because of *His work*, not your own, that your sin is no longer a barrier between you and Him. By His grace, you can now be in His presence. Being holy means being set apart for God's exclusive purposes. God calls you to be holy as a way of life. "In the past you did not have the understanding you have now, so you did the evil things you wanted to do. But now you are children of God, so you should obey Him and not live the way you did before. Be holy in everything you do, just as God is holy. He is the one who chose you. In the Scriptures God says, 'Be holy, because I am holy.'" "You also are like living stones, and God is using you to build a spiritual house. You are

> God's ongoing work in us to make us holy starts at the moment of our salvation and continues throughout our lives, making us a little more like Jesus every day.

14 Hebrews 10:10.

15 1 Peter 1:14–16.

to serve God in this house as holy priests, offering Him spiritual sacrifices that He will accept because of Jesus Christ." [16]

Think of God's character. His character is holy in that it is perfect, pure, and without sin. We are to reflect His character by striving for holiness in all we do. "We should make ourselves pure—free from anything that makes our body or our soul unclean. Our respect for God should make us try to be completely holy in the way we live." [17] We honor God by striving always toward holiness with our words, actions, and thoughts.

Sanctification: The act of God's grace by which the affections of men are purified or alienated from sin and the world, and exalted to a supreme love to God.

But holiness is more about who we are in Christ than the things we do. The Holy Spirit sanctifies us, meaning He changes us on the inside, making us holy like He is. *Sanctification*, or God's ongoing work in us to make us holy, starts at the moment of our salvation and continues throughout our lives, making us a little more like Jesus every day.

The life of holiness starts when we hear the good news of Jesus's free offer of salvation, believe, confess our sins, repent, and get baptized. And it does not stop there. For the rest of our lives, we continue to learn and grow in our faith, confessing sin and repenting when needed. We are all works in progress, growing little by little—and sometimes all at once—until the day we die and enter into a new phase of our life with God.

[16] 1 Peter 2:5, 9.

[17] 2 Corinthians 7:1.

How can you cooperate with the Holy Spirit of God working in you so that you can become more holy day by day?

_____

_____

_____

_____

_____

God's Work in Us

We are called to be holy, and it is God's transforming work in us that makes us holy. Many Christians speak of the radical changes they go through once they are saved. For some, the changes seem to take place suddenly—from one day to the next. For others, the process is slower and more gradual. They may go from using foul language to hating foul language. They may suddenly be able to step away from drugs and other addictions. They may go from being depressed to discovering joy. These are examples of the miraculous power of the Holy Spirit sanctifying us.

Imagine for a moment that you have been selected to be part of an Olympic team, representing your nation before the entire world. As an athlete preparing for the Olympics, I'm sure you would bring all your attention, dedication, and commitment to your goal because you have been *set apart* for that purpose. You are willing to sacrifice the momentary pleasures of junk food, sleeping late, and being lazy. You do things that others won't do because you are set apart for that special purpose.

So it is with your life in Christ. You are "to present your bodies as a living sacrifice, holy and acceptable to God, which is your spiritual worship." [18] As followers of Jesus, you say no to sin. You aim for holiness, and the Holy Spirit does the work. "All who compete in the games use strict training. They do this so that they can win a prize—one that doesn't last. But our prize is one that will last forever." [19] "Let us run with endurance the race God has set before us." [20]

Sometimes your progress toward holiness may seem slow, or you may even find yourself taking a step backwards. This is a time to stop and reflect on where you are and where you are going. How did you get off the path? It might be time to repent, confess, or make amends. Ask for help from God and from trusted Christian friends. It is never too late and you are never too far gone to get back on the path. "And I am certain that God, who began the good work within you, will continue His work until it is finally finished on the day when Christ Jesus returns." [21]

> **When you fall off the path of holiness, what are two things you can do to pick yourself up and get back on the path?**
>
> _____
>
> _____

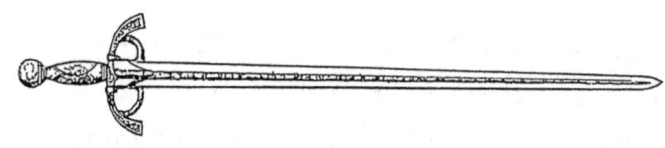

---

[18] Romans 12:1, ESV.

[19] 1 Corinthians 9:25.

[20] Hebrews 12:1, NLT.

[21] Philippians 1:6, NLT.

A LIFE OF SHARING THE GOOD NEWS

One of the things Jesus specifically calls you to do as a Christian is to share the *gospel*—a word that means "good news." This call is what is known as the Great Commission, and the act of sharing the gospel is called *evangelism*. Jesus says it like this: "Go and make followers of all people in the world. Baptize them in the name of the Father and the Son and the Holy Spirit. Teach them to obey everything that I have told you to do."[22]

Gospel: The history of the birth, life, actions, death, resurrection, ascension and doctrines of Jesus Christ; or a revelation of the grace of God to fallen man through a mediator, including the character, actions, and doctrines of Christ, with the whole scheme of salvation, as revealed by Christ and His apostles.

For, "'everyone who calls on the name of the LORD will be saved.' But how can they call on Him to save them unless they believe in Him? And how can they believe in Him if they have never heard about Him? And how can they hear about Him unless someone tells them? And how will anyone go and tell them without

---

[22] Matthew 28:19–20.

being sent? That is why the Scriptures say, 'How beautiful are the feet of messengers who bring good news!'"[23]

This quote about the beautiful feet refers to the Old Testament prophet Isaiah. He said, "How beautiful on the mountains are the feet of the messenger who brings good news, the good news of peace and salvation, the news that the God of Israel reigns!"[24]

In the wars of ancient times, a runner would be sent from the front lines of battle to deliver news to the generals about how the war was progressing. When the war was won, the final news of victory that the runner delivered was called the "good news," or the "gospel." Victory in battle was good news indeed, and the feet of the person bearing that news were considered beautiful!

You have some very good news to share about a battle that has been won. In fact, it is the best news of all! This good news is that death and sin have been defeated, and Jesus is the Victorious Warrior in this battle. It is not a battle against flesh and blood but "against the spiritual powers of evil in the heavenly places."[25] The good news is that God, the Ruler of the universe, loved the world so much He sent His Son to live as a man and die for our sins, in fulfillment of the Scriptures. He was crucified, died, was buried, and rose again from the dead. He ascended to the right hand of the Father in heaven and will return one day to establish His kingdom forever. If we believe in this gospel, we will be saved and will live forever with Him. It's that simple.

You get to be a part of spreading this joyous news of Jesus's victory. Are you ready to be a runner that takes this good news to "explain about the hope you have"[26] in Christ Jesus? An effective way to share the gospel with others is to prepare your personal story, or your testimony, of how you came to Christ. You can have a short version—one that takes three minutes to tell

---

23 Romans 10:13–15, NLT.

24 Isaiah 52:7, NLT.

25 Ephesians 6:12.

26 1 Peter 3:15.

(some people call this the "elevator" version because you can share it with a stranger in the time it takes to ride with that person in an elevator)—and a longer version for those people who want to hear more. You should write down your testimony and memorize it so it is on the tip of your tongue when you need it. This way, you can be ready to share the good news of what Jesus has done in your life anywhere and anytime. Many people are just waiting for someone to share this good news with them. They may appear to have their lives together and not have a care in the world, but inside they may be unfulfilled and ready to receive your testimony with joy. You never know how God may use you, so it is best to always be ready.

Memorize 1 Peter 3:15 in any version. Here is one you can use:

"But in your hearts honor Christ the Lord as holy, always being prepared to make a defense to anyone who asks you for a reason for the hope that is in you; yet do it with gentleness and respect."[27]

In time, sharing your testimony will become second nature to you, and you can add new details and Scriptures. Christians many times wear the joy of Messiah on their faces and in their behavior, leading others to ask, "What is the source of your joy?" Can you imagine someone looking at you and wanting the joy you have? What a privilege to be Jesus's ambassador to the world! We will speak more about your testimony later in this book.

---

[27] 1 Peter 3:15, ESV.

You can share the gospel in words, but you also represent Jesus even when you are not speaking to anyone. When you profess Christ, the world is watching you. Your life and the way you act reflect on Him and the gospel message. Your character is part of your evangelism. Even the things you say or the way you act in your unguarded moments can impact people's lives. Your peace, joy, and good deeds reflect well on Jesus and on Christians and can attract others to Jesus. And, likewise, those who call themselves Christians yet do not act in a Christlike manner can keep others from accepting the message of the gospel.

You may have the blessing of leading someone to accept Jesus as their Savior. And what a wonderful blessing that is! Here is an example of a prayer you can share with a person who might be wondering how to become a Christian. You can assure that person that "if you openly declare that Jesus is Lord and believe in your heart that God raised Him from the dead, you will be saved."[28] You might ask them to say something like this:

> *Jesus, I believe that You are Lord and that You rose from the dead to give me life. Please forgive my sins and make me a new creature. Come and live in my heart and show me how to live.*

If they truly believe, then Jesus will honor their confession of faith. Now you can welcome them into the kingdom of God as your brother or sister in Christ and begin to teach them the things you are learning. You can invite them to join you at your church. You become a disciple discipling others!

Make a list of all the people with whom you would like one day to share the good news of Jesus Christ. Pray that God would give you boldness to step out and do it. Pick one and bravely share with that person this week. That is the beginning of your life of sharing the good news!

_____   _____

_____   _____

_____   _____

---

[28] Romans 10:9, NLT.

A LIFE OF WORSHIP

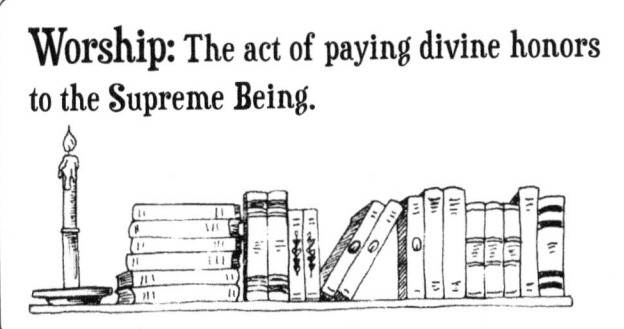

Worship: The act of paying divine honors to the Supreme Being.

To be a Christian is to live a life of worship. *Worship* is honor, reverence, respect, and devotion, and it is the natural response to our awesome God. Think about it— God created the universe. Can we even imagine the size of the universe? We live on a planet that revolves around our sun. Our sun is but one of 100 billion stars in our Milky Way galaxy. And our galaxy is but one of as many as two trillion galaxies in the observable universe. But the observable universe is estimated at only 3 percent of the entire universe. And that is all merely a twinkle in God's eye! God is so great that He holds our universe in the palm of His hand. If the universe is impossible to grasp, how much further beyond our understanding is the One who created it!

God keeps the planets in orbit and at the same time knows every hair on our heads.

God keeps the planets in orbit and at the same time knows every hair on our heads. He knows the past, present, and future. And He knows what is best for each and every one of us. God is awesome not just for what He has done for us out of His great heart of love but for *who He is.* "Oh, how great are God's riches and wisdom and knowledge! How impossible it is for us to understand His decisions and His ways!"[29] The reverence that wells up in us when we stop to think about all this cannot help but cause us to worship Him, as is His due.

Even the angels in heaven cannot help but bow down and worship God. "You are God. LORD, only You are God. You made the sky and the highest heavens and everything in them. You made the earth and everything on it. You made the seas and everything in them. You give life to everything. All the heavenly angels bow down and worship You."[30]

On top of all that, consider God's amazing love for humanity that caused Him to send His Son from His lofty heavenly throne to become one of us—a human being. Realizing His unlimited love for us only deepens our worship. Many times in the Old Testament, you will find that when people worship God, they bow down to the ground. This is a way of showing humility and respect before God. "Then all the people bowed down and put their faces low to the ground and they worshiped the LORD."[31]

Worship can take many forms. It can be expressed in prayer, in singing, in dancing, and truly in all you do. It can take place in your secret prayer closet or in a stadium with hundreds of other worshippers. You can use lots of words, or you can just groan, knowing that the Lord searches your heart. Worship can be formal, according to your church's set patterns, or it can be spontaneous and continuous—any time of day or night regardless of the circumstances. Think about this idea: let everything you do be an act of worship.

On a separate piece of paper, write a letter to God and tell Him how wonderful He is to you.

---

[29] Romans 11:33, NLT.

[30] Nehemiah 9:6.

[31] Nehemiah 8:6.

God Desires Our Worship

When God set the slaves free from bondage in Egypt, the reason He gave for His action was so that they could "go worship Him in the desert." [32] God desires our worship because our worship shows that we have a proper understanding of who He is and who we are in relation to Him. "The LORD enjoys people who worship Him and trust in His faithful love." [33] He knows that we are weak and easily deceived, and He is very concerned that our worship be directed at Him and not at false gods. In the ten commandments, God says, "Don't worship or serve idols of any kind, because I, the LORD, am your God. I hate My people worshiping other gods." [34]

As a Christian, you already know that Jesus is Lord and that without His sacrifice, you would be left dead in your sins. You know that He is worthy of all your worship, honor, and praise. The words of the Bible offer a great starting point for you to express your worship of God. Looking to the example of the Bible authors, here are some of Moses's words of worship: "Lord, You have been our dwelling place in all generations. Before the mountains were brought forth, or ever You had formed the earth and the world, from everlasting to everlasting You are God." [35]

Here is an example of how King David worshiped God through his poetic psalms: "The Lord can be trusted in all that He says. He is loyal in all that He does. The

---

[32] Exodus 7:16.

[33] Psalm 147:11.

[34] Exodus 20:5.

[35] Psalm 90:1–2, ESV.

> Lord, You have been our dwelling place in all generations. Before the mountains were brought forth, or ever You had formed the earth and the world, from everlasting to everlasting You are God.

Lord lifts up people who have fallen. He helps those who are in trouble. All living things look to You for their food, and You give them their food at the right time. You open Your hands and give every living thing all that it needs. Everything the Lord does is good."[36]

Another example of worship comes from a grateful blind man Jesus healed: "He bowed down at Jesus' feet and thanked Him."[37] Your thanksgiving is also part of your life of worship.

In the Bible, we get a view of the heavenly realm where God dwells. He allowed some of His prophets to see that holy place and record what they saw. For example, God gave the prophet Isaiah a view of His throne room. What were the heavenly beings doing in God's throne room? Isaiah says that "the angels were calling to each other, 'Holy, holy, holy is the LORD All-Powerful. His Glory fills the whole earth.'"[38]

They were *worshiping God.*

John, the disciple of Jesus, also got a view of God's throne room, recorded in the book of Revelation, the last book of the Bible. What were the heavenly beings doing there? John says that "day and night they never stopped

---

[36] Psalm 145:13–17.

[37] Luke 17:16.

[38] Isaiah 6:3.

saying, 'Holy, holy, holy is the Lord God All-Powerful. He always was, He is, and He is coming.'"[39] "Then I looked, and there was a large crowd of people. There were so many people that no one could count them all. They were from every nation, tribe, race of people, and language of the earth. They were standing before the throne and before the Lamb. They all wore white robes and had palm branches in their hands. They shouted loudly, 'Victory belongs to our God, who sits on the throne, and to the Lamb.'... The angels bowed down on their faces before the throne and worshiped God. They said, 'Amen! Praise, glory, wisdom, thanks, honor, power, and strength belong to our God forever and ever. Amen!'"[40]

They, too, were *worshiping God*. They are probably worshiping God in His heavenly dwelling place right this moment!

It is very likely that after this life is over, our everlasting life with God will be a life of worship—not because we have to out of obligation but because we want nothing more than to give God the praise, honor, glory, and adoration due Him. That is a natural response in the face of our holy God. Worship will not be a boring activity. The excitement and effect of being in the presence of God will fill us with awe at His magnificence and overwhelming joy such that we will want to do nothing else but worship.

---

[39] Revelation 4:8.

[40] Revelation 7:9–12.

The Bible says that the heavenly beings before the throne of God never stop worshiping Him "day and night." What do you think they know that causes them to do this?

_____

_____

_____

_____

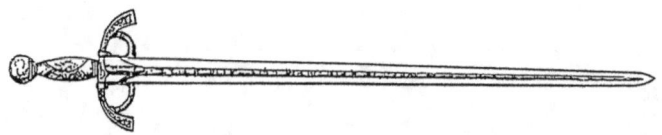

A LIFE OF PURITY

"Fix your thoughts on what is true, and honorable, and right, and pure, and lovely, and admirable."[41]

The process of becoming spiritually pure is much like refining silver or gold. These metals must go through high heat to burn off impurities. It is by exposure to the high heat of God's testing that He purifies us. Sometimes this can be uncomfortable when, under the fire of God's testing, we come to see behaviors and qualities we need to leave behind. But it is for our good that God purifies us. "Fire is used to make gold and silver pure, but a person's heart is made pure by the LORD."[42]

> ## Your life takes place in a God-given body, and you want that body to be a place of purity.

Your body is a place for God to reside. It is "a temple for the Holy Spirit that you received from God and that lives in you. You don't own yourselves."[43] Your life takes place in a God-given body, and you want that body to be a place of purity.

One challenging area where people often struggle to be spiritually pure is in their sexuality. Many are tempted by physical desires to have sex outside of marriage. Sex

---

[41] Philippians 4:8, NLT.

[42] Proverbs 17:3.

[43] 1 Corinthians 6:19.

was designed by God to take place within marriage. It is a holy, God-ordained gift of love between husband and wife. It builds intimacy, brings children into the world, grows family, and strengthens the marriage bond. Sex outside of marriage is impure and not what God has for you. It is an abuse of the precious gift that God ordains for husband and wife alone.

The process of being purified by God can be unpleasant, as we find we have to stare our impurities in the face and become willing to let them go. Are you willing to allow God to purify you?

_____

_____

Before Marriage

The unmarried Christian is bombarded with messages from the world that encourage self-indulgence. These messages come at us from our smartphones, computers, pop songs, movies, and other media, selling the idea that it is good to satisfy our appetites. "Go for it!" "YOLO—You only live once!" *But know*: this is the message of the enemy of God. Self-restraint is the way of the Christian. We do not act on our impulses. We act prayerfully, with an eye toward how we can be pure vessels for God. King David asks, "Who can go up on the LORD's mountain? Who can stand in His holy Temple? Only those who have not done evil, who have pure hearts."[44]

Sex before marriage, or fornication, disrespects our bodies, our dignity, and the one we have sex with. It also places the young woman at risk of becoming pregnant. This is when she may make the terrible and tragic mistake of aborting her child, which not only takes the life of her child but leaves her with lifelong scars.

A life of purity before marriage means setting boundaries and using self-control. Unmarried Christians must pray that the Holy Spirit gives them

---

[44] Psalm 24:3–4.

self-control, which is one of the fruits of the Spirit.[45] The man and woman who honor God's leading in the area of their sexuality will enjoy the beautiful reward of dignity that comes from respecting their bodies as God intended.

> # Those who honor God's leading in the area of their sexuality will enjoy the beautiful reward of dignity that comes from respecting their bodies as God intended.

The Bible says: "Now in a great house there are not only vessels of gold and silver but also of wood and clay, some for honorable use, some for dishonorable. Therefore, if anyone cleanses himself from what is dishonorable, he will be a vessel for honorable use, set apart as holy, useful to the master of the house, ready for every good work."[46]

Vessels: Ministers of the gospel, as appointed to bear the glad news of salvation to others.

[45] Read about the fruit of the Spirit at Galatians 5:22–23.

[46] 2 Timothy 2:20–21, ESV.

The word *vessel* is defined as a container for holding something. It is also defined as a person in whom some quality is contained. If you think of yourself as a vessel, what qualities would you like to contain?

_____

_____

_____

_____

In Marriage

Self-control plays a big role in guiding the Christian toward purity before marriage, but what about once you are married? Self-control is still important. Christian marriage is sacred, and its purity must be guarded. Marriage is a reflection of God's relationship with His church. Jesus "gave Himself up for her, that He might sanctify her, having cleansed her by the washing of water with the Word, so that He might present the church to Himself in splendor, without spot or wrinkle or any such thing, that she might be holy and without blemish."[47] In Christian marriage, we are to remember that we reflect Jesus's marriage to His beloved church. With that sacred example in mind, we are to treat our marriages and our spouses with the utmost care and respect.

When we get married, we get a license from a government office. But when we enter into a Christian marriage, we make a sacred covenant and stand not just before the government but before God. God is included in our vows and our married life.

The husband and wife become one flesh in a holy, God-made union. Jesus says that husband and wife "are no longer two, but one. God has joined them together, so no one should separate them."[48] They must guard against

---

[47] Ephesians 5:25–27.

[48] Matthew 19:6.

anything that gets in the way of their oneness. God does not want His holy institution of marriage to be made impure by unfaithfulness of any kind. "The LORD, the God of Israel, says, 'I hate divorce, and I hate the cruel things that men do. So protect your spiritual unity. Don't cheat on your wife.'"[49]

"Wives, submit to your own husbands, as to the Lord.... Husbands, love your wives, just as Christ also loved the church and gave Himself for her."[50] The husband and the wife are to love each other sacrificially in mutual submission, "as to the Lord" and "just as Christ also loved the church." Christ loved the church so much He gave His life for her.

God created man and woman equally in His image. "So God created humans in His own image. He created them to be like Himself. He created them male and female."[51] Each has a role. Neither role is more important than the other but is only different in kind. A

> **A pure marriage is one where husband and wife serve one another with mutual respect and gentleness, both looking to Jesus as their authority.**

[49] Malachi 2:16.

[50] Ephesians 5:22, 25, NKJV.

[51] Genesis 1:27.

pure marriage is one where husband and wife serve one another with mutual respect and gentleness, both looking to Jesus as their authority.

Not everyone is married, and some will never marry. The Bible says that it is a gift for some to remain single. The single person is also called to purity. In all we think and do—our eating, the music we listen to, the social media we consume, the words that come out of our mouths, and all things we allow to enter through our eyes and ears—our Christian character should be aiming toward purity. Jesus is our model of purity. "We know that when Christ comes again, we will be like Him. We will see Him just as He is. He is pure, and everyone who has this hope in Him keeps themselves pure like Christ."[52]

Do you have a role model that you can look to as an example of purity in marriage or in living the Christian life? What can you learn from that person that you can apply to your own pursuit of purity?

_____

_____

_____

_____

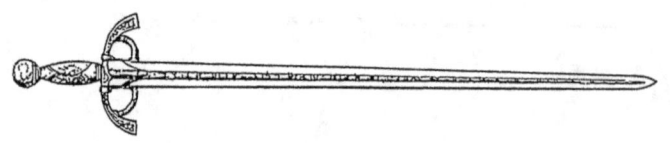

---

[52] 1 John 3:2–3.

A LIFE OF STEWARDSHIP

When God created humans, He told them to be fruitful and multiply. He also said, "Fill the earth and subdue it, and have dominion over the fish of the sea and over the birds of the heavens and over every living thing that moves on the earth."[53] What does this mean? It means He wanted them to take responsibility and be good stewards over His creation. What is a steward? It is a caretaker. God created a beautiful earth for us to live on. While we love God's creation, we must not make the mistake of worshiping the creation. We worship the Creator and show honor to Him by taking excellent care of His creation. We are to be earth's stewards, caring for His creation with love and attention to maintain its beauty and productivity.

> # We worship the Creator and show honor to Him by taking excellent care of His creation.

"The LORD God placed the man in the Garden of Eden to tend and watch over it."[54] He expected Adam to work the garden as a steward: to guard it and tend to it. Adam was to shape the land so it could be productive and continually useful. That meant that Adam was expected to work hard and take responsibility.

[53] Genesis 1:28, ESV.

[54] Genesis 2:15, NLT.

We are to do the same. We are to remember that "the earth and everything on it belong to the LORD. The world and all its people belong to Him. He built the earth on the water. He built it over the rivers."[55] Caring for God's creation and managing the blessings He gives us from out of His abundance are ways we honor Him. Stewards do not own the things they manage. They are responsible to the owner to manage his things well. The owner of all our blessings is God.

We are to be responsible in caring for all the resources God places in our hands to manage. For some of us, the task of being a good steward could mean managing our money, using our time effectively, respecting the natural environment, or raising children to be contributing members of society. There are many ways we can show good stewardship. Whenever God gives us a blessing of any kind, we are to manage it well.

What is one area of blessing God has given you to steward with excellence?

_____

_____

_____

Stewardship of Money

There is a common idea among some Christians that money and profit are evil, but that is not what the Bible says. The Bible says that "the love of money is the root of all kinds of evil."[56] Notice, it is "the _love of money_" that is the problem. There is nothing wrong with earning, saving, making profit, spending, and giving. After all, it is hard to be a charitable giver from an empty pocket.

Good stewardship of money means that whatever you earn, you remember that your abundance comes from God and you are to manage it wisely.

---

55 Psalm 24:1–2.

56 1 Timothy 6:10, NLT.

> **True wealth is found in following Jesus and placing nothing above Him. Our salvation and relationship with Jesus are our treasures.**

True wealth is found in following Jesus and placing nothing above Him. Our salvation and relationship with Jesus are our treasures. "Don't save treasures for yourselves here on earth. Moths and rust will destroy them. And thieves can break into your house and steal them. Instead, save your treasures in heaven, where they cannot be destroyed by moths or rust and where thieves cannot break in and steal them. Your heart will be where your treasure is."[57]

Still, we need money to live. In many stories that Jesus tells about money, there is a recurring message of the need to be good stewards of that money. We are expected to be responsible in our handling of money.

- We must not gamble or spend frivolously.
- We should be careful not to spend money we do not have, such as when we use credit cards. "The one who borrows is a slave to the one who lends."[58] God does not want us enslaved in that way.

---

[57] Matthew 6:19–21.

[58] Proverbs 22:7.

- If we want or need something, it is best to save up for it rather than getting a loan from a bank. A wise steward of money stays free of debt and takes care to save for the future. (Exceptions can be made when the loan is "secured" by something like a car or a house. In that case, the car or house has value equal to the debt.)

- We should plan ahead and budget our funds so we don't end up with "too much month at the end of the money." Budgeting is our way of knowing exactly how much money is coming in and how much is being spent each month. We plan so we will always have what we need when we need it.

It is never too late to develop good money-management habits. As a young person, you have a unique gift: that is the gift of time. If you begin saving money and put it in a secure bank that pays interest, it will grow in time. And then there will be interest on the interest. This is called *compound interest*.

Here is something to consider: Let's say that two young people of the same age earn the same amount of money, and the first person starts saving when he is twenty. He puts the same amount each month into a bank account and stops saving when he is thirty. He leaves the money in the bank, earning compound interest.

The second person starts saving when she is thirty, putting that same amount in the bank each month until retirement age. When these two reach retirement age, the first person will have more money in savings than the one who saved her whole life but started ten years later. This is because of the power of compound interest working over time. A wise steward takes advantage of this.

Here is a sample budget you can use to start planning how you manage your money. Use it as an example and create your own budget based on your needs. You can't get control of your money without knowing exactly where it is going.

Budget for the month of:			
Income	Amount	Expenses	Amount
Pay		Rent	
Gifts		Groceries	
Extra Work		Fuel	
(etc.)		(etc.)	
		Savings	
		Tithes	
Income Total:		Expenses Total:	
Income - Expenses =			

What Is Tithing?

Tithing is the practice of giving 10 percent of all your earnings to your church. This practice was first seen in the Bible when the patriarch Abraham "gave Melchizedek one-tenth of everything."[59] Melchizedek was "a priest of God Most High."[60] Your tithing shows that you trust in God as the source of all your financial blessings. Tithing is a spiritual act—a form of worship. It shows your good stewardship and faith in God.

> # Tithing is a form of worship and a demonstration of your good stewardship and your faith.

[59] Genesis 14:20.

[60] Genesis 14:18.

Giving is a great joy, and you can give above and beyond your tithes. "You will have a greater blessing when you give than when you receive."[61] One way to show God your appreciation for the blessings He pours out is to share those blessings in the form of offerings to your church or those in need. Jesus once taught in this way: "When you give a lunch or a dinner, don't invite only your friends, brothers, relatives, and rich neighbors. At another time they will pay you back by inviting you to eat with them. Instead, when you give a feast, invite the poor, the crippled, and the blind. Then you will have great blessings, because these people cannot pay you back. They have nothing. But God will reward you at the time when all godly people rise from death."[62]

Sometimes, you might be reluctant to tithe and give offerings because you do not want to part with your hard-earned money. Tithing and giving are acts of faith in God and His provision. "This same God who takes care of me will supply all your needs from His glorious riches, which have been given to us in Christ Jesus."[63] Step forward in faith that God knows your needs. In the Bible, God says to "bring all the tithes into the storehouse, that there may be food in My house, and try Me now in this, … If I will not open for you the windows of heaven and pour out for you such blessing that there will not be room enough to receive it."[64] Wise stewards walk in faith, knowing that all their provision comes from the Lord and planning to tithe and save as part of their budgeting.

Talk about a time when you enjoyed giving more than receiving.

_____

_____

_____

---

[61] Acts 20:35.

[62] Luke 14:12–14.

[63] Philippians 4:19, NLT.

[64] Malachi 3:10, NKJV.

A LIFE OF STUDY

The life of the Christian is a life of study. The Bible tells us that when the apostle Paul met with a certain community of believers called the Bereans, they were special because they "studied the Scriptures every day to make sure that what they heard was really true. The result was that many of them believed."[65]

The people of Berea were famous in the New Testament church because they "studied the Scriptures every day." They did this to be sure that what the apostle Paul was teaching them was true. Of course, they did not have the New Testament, like you do, because it had not yet been written. They searched the Old Testament and saw in it the prophecies and the "types and shadows" that pointed to Jesus. They saw for themselves the truth of the gospel that Paul had been teaching them concerning Jesus. And the truth set them free.

Let's all be like the Bereans and study the Bible daily. There are so many rich treasures to be found in the Bible that a lifetime of study could not exhaust them. The most advanced scholars in all the world can never reach the end of all there is to learn. It is a good practice to find teachers—Christians who have studied the Bible more than you—to help you understand those things that may be confusing to you.

When you study the Bible diligently and with prayer, in time, the Holy Spirit reveals to you the truth of the character of God and His plan for humanity. Even though the Bible is not written like a textbook, the big picture of God's salvation plan comes into focus as you read

[65] Acts 17:11–12.

through it and make the connections. As you read, you can put together pieces almost like a puzzle. Together, the pieces reveal His grand story.

> **As you read, you can put together pieces like a puzzle to eventually reveal His grand story.**

How can you be like the Bereans?

_____

_____

_____

The Parables of Jesus

Many times when Jesus taught, He used stories, or parables, to make His points. We do not read the stories in the parables as historical events. Instead, we read them as lessons to help us understand His kingdom and its principles. The word *parable* refers to a comparison, symbol, or type. For example, Jesus said, "God's kingdom is like a mustard seed that a man plants in his field. It is the smallest of all seeds. But when it grows, it is the largest of all garden plants. It becomes a tree big enough for the birds to come and make nests in its branches."[66]

In this parable, Jesus makes a comparison between something we are familiar with in the physical world (a tiny mustard seed) and something we can't see with our physical eyes (God's kingdom). This parable is Jesus's way of saying that a small spiritual beginning can become great through the power of God.

Types and Shadows

We mentioned types and shadows above. What are they? Types and shadows are teaching pictures of things to come. For example, Paul used the word

---

[66] Matthew 13:31–32.

type when he spoke of Adam as "*a type* of Him who was to come"[67]—that is, Jesus. Paul meant that Adam was a blueprint, or a sketch, of someone greater who was to come at a later time. That someone was Jesus.

The writer of the book of Hebrews used the words *sketch* and *shadow* when he spoke of the tabernacle in the wilderness as but a "*sketch* and *shadow* of the heavenly sanctuary."[68] In other words, God instructed Moses to build a place of worship here on earth that was patterned after the more perfect tabernacle in the heavens where God dwells.

> # Your shadow is not your body, but it tells a lot about your body.

If you stand in the sunlight during the day, your body will cast a shadow. This shadow is not your body, but it tells a lot about your body—your size, shape, and location, for example. So it is with God's teaching pictures. They point to something, or someone (Jesus), more important than they are. Keep your spiritual eyes open for how Jesus is pictured and prophesied from the very first pages of the Old Testament, even though the Old Testament was written long before Jesus was born as a man. God planted seeds of knowledge about our coming Savior throughout His book, and you can be the treasure hunter, finding types and shadows that reveal who Jesus is and putting the puzzle pieces in place.

---

67 Romans 5:14, NKJV.

68 Hebrews 8:5, NEW ENGLISH TRANSLATION (NET).

Go out and stand in the sunshine. Look at your shadow. What information about yourself can you get from looking at your shadow?

_____

_____

_____

_____

Prophecy and Fulfillment

Below, you can read for yourself some prophecies from the Old Testament, long before Jesus lived as a man, and the fulfillment of those prophecies in the New Testament in the person of Jesus.

Jesus ...	Old Testament Prophecy	New Testament Fulfillment
Was born in Bethlehem	Micah 5:2	Matthew 2:1; Luke 2:4–7
Was born of a virgin	Isaiah 7:14	Matthew 1:21–23
Was from the tribe of Judah	Genesis 49:10	Luke 3:23, 33; Hebrews 7:14
Was taken to Egypt	Hosea 11:1	Matthew 2:14–15
Performed miracles	Isaiah 35:5–6	Matthew 9:35
Cleansed the Temple	Malachi 3:1	Matthew 21:12–13
Entered Jerusalem as a king on a donkey	Zechariah 9:9	Matthew 21:4–9
Was rejected by His people	Isaiah 53:3	John 1:11
Died a humiliating death involving:	–	–

Jesus ...	Old Testament Prophecy	New Testament Fulfillment
• betrayal by a friend	Psalm 41:9	Luke 22:3–4; John 13:18
• being sold for thirty pieces of silver	Zechariah 11:12	Matthew 26:14–15
• silence before His accusers	Isaiah 53:7	Matthew 27:12–14
• being mocked	Psalm 22:7–8	Matthew 27:31
• being beaten	Isaiah 52:14	Matthew 27:26
• being spit upon	Isaiah 50:6	Matthew 27:30
• piercing of His hands and feet	Psalm 22:16	Matthew 27:31; John 20:25
• being crucified with thieves	Isaiah 53:12	Matthew 27:38
• dying for His persecutors	Isaiah 53:12	Luke 23:34
• piercing His side	Zechariah 12:10	John 19:34
• gall and vinegar to drink	Psalm 69:21	Matthew 27:34, Luke 23:36
• no broken bones	Psalm 34:20	John 19:32–36
• being buried in a rich man's tomb	Isaiah 53:9	Matthew 27:57–60
• lots cast for His garments	Psalm 22:18	John 19:23–24
Rose from the dead!	Psalm 16:10; Isaiah 53:10	Mark 16:6; Acts 2:31
Ascended to heaven	Psalm 68:18	Acts 1:9
Sat down at the right hand of God	Psalm 110:1	Heb 1:3

After reading these examples, pick a few and discuss.

_____

_____

_____

_____

_____

More Teaching Pictures

Aside from these prophecies, as you read the Bible, look for other ways that God teaches about Jesus. One example is the story of Abraham's sacrifice of his son Isaac. Here, we see a father willing to give up his son as a sacrifice. This is a teaching picture of God's greater sacrifice of His Son, which was to come more than two thousand years later. Isaac was willing to obey his father. This pictures Jesus's willingness to obey His Father and go to the cross.

God does not require human sacrifice. He requires obedience. Abraham and Isaac were obedient. God stopped Abraham from going through with the sacrifice of Isaac and instead provided a substitute in the form of a ram. [69] Much later, He provided the ultimate substitute in the person of His Son, Jesus, and Jesus "humbled Himself by being fully obedient to God, even when that caused His death—death on a cross." [70]

We see another teaching picture in the tabernacle and temple sacrifices in the Old Testament that atoned for sin through the shedding of the blood of spotless animals. To _atone_ means to pay for a crime or sin. The Bible explains, "For the life of the flesh is in the blood, and I [God] have given it to you on the altar to make atonement for your souls; for it is the blood by reason of the life that makes atonement." [71]

---

[69] Read this story in Genesis 22.

[70] Philippians 2:8.

[71] Leviticus 17:11, NASB.

132

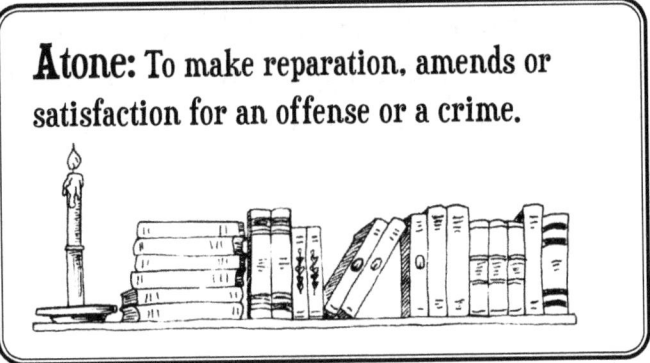

Atone: To make reparation, amends or satisfaction for an offense or a crime.

As you read about the different animal sacrifices, you can see that they all point as teaching pictures to the once-for-all-time perfect offering that was to come in the spotless Lamb, Jesus. "Christ offered Himself through the eternal Spirit as a perfect sacrifice to God. His blood will make us completely clean from the evil we have done. It will give us clear consciences so that we can worship the living God."[72]

The following is a small sample of more teaching pictures you can explore on your own. Read them and the Scriptures that go with them and consider the questions:

- When the people become so wicked on the earth that God wants to destroy them in a flood, He finds one man who is righteous—Noah. He gives Noah and his family a way to escape destruction. God tells Noah to build an ark that will withstand the terrible flood. Noah believes God and builds the ark even though everyone laughs at him. "Noah pleased the LORD" (Found in Genesis 6–9).

What does Noah's ark teach us about being in the safety of God's plan of salvation through faith in Him?

---

[72] Hebrews 9:14.

- When we look at the life of Joseph, we see a teaching picture of the life of Jesus. Like Jesus, Joseph is beloved by his father and rejected by his brothers. He becomes the one who saves his people (Found in Genesis 37; 39–50).

How does Joseph remind you of Jesus?

- When Moses is sent to free God's people from slavery in Egypt, we see Jesus pictured in the Passover event as a spotless lamb whose blood protects people from destruction (Found in Exodus 12).

How is the Passover lamb a teaching picture of Jesus?

- In Isaiah 52–53, we find a teaching picture of a Suffering Servant who would one day come. This coming one suffers not for himself but for the sins of others. He dies yet lives after he dies (Found in Isaiah 52:13–53:12).

How does the Suffering Servant remind you of Jesus?

- Some of the teaching pictures we find in the Old Testament were spoken of by Jesus Himself. One example of this is the story of Jonah. Jesus tells us, "Jonah was in the stomach of the big fish for three days and three nights. In the same way, the Son of Man will be in the grave three days and three nights"[73] (Read Jonah 1).

Why do you think Jesus compared Himself to Jonah?

As you live a life of study, God's Word hidden in your heart will act as insurance against sin, and you will be able to say with confidence: "I have hidden Your word in my heart, that I might not sin against You."[74] It will be "a lamp that guides my steps, a light that shows the path I should take."[75]

---

[73] Matthew 12:40.

[74] Psalm 119:11, NLT.

[75] Psalm 119:105.

As you live a life of study, not only will you learn about God and His great plan but you will also find life lessons that will seem like they were written just for you and just when you need them. Ask of the Holy Spirit "that the eyes of your heart may be enlightened." [76] Jesus promises that the Holy Spirit "will lead you into all truth." [77] This is a precious promise that will bring you a lifetime of joy.

MORE TO DISCUSS

1.   **A**s you learn about living the Christian life, name three things you want to change in your life in order to be more in line with God's purposes.

2. Who in the Bible do you look to most as a role model and example of godly living? Jesus is an obvious answer, but who else can you name and why?

3. What do you find most difficult and challenging about living the Christian life?

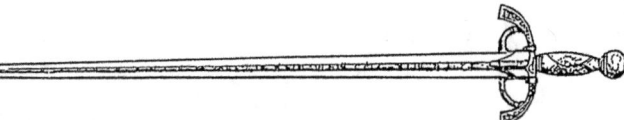

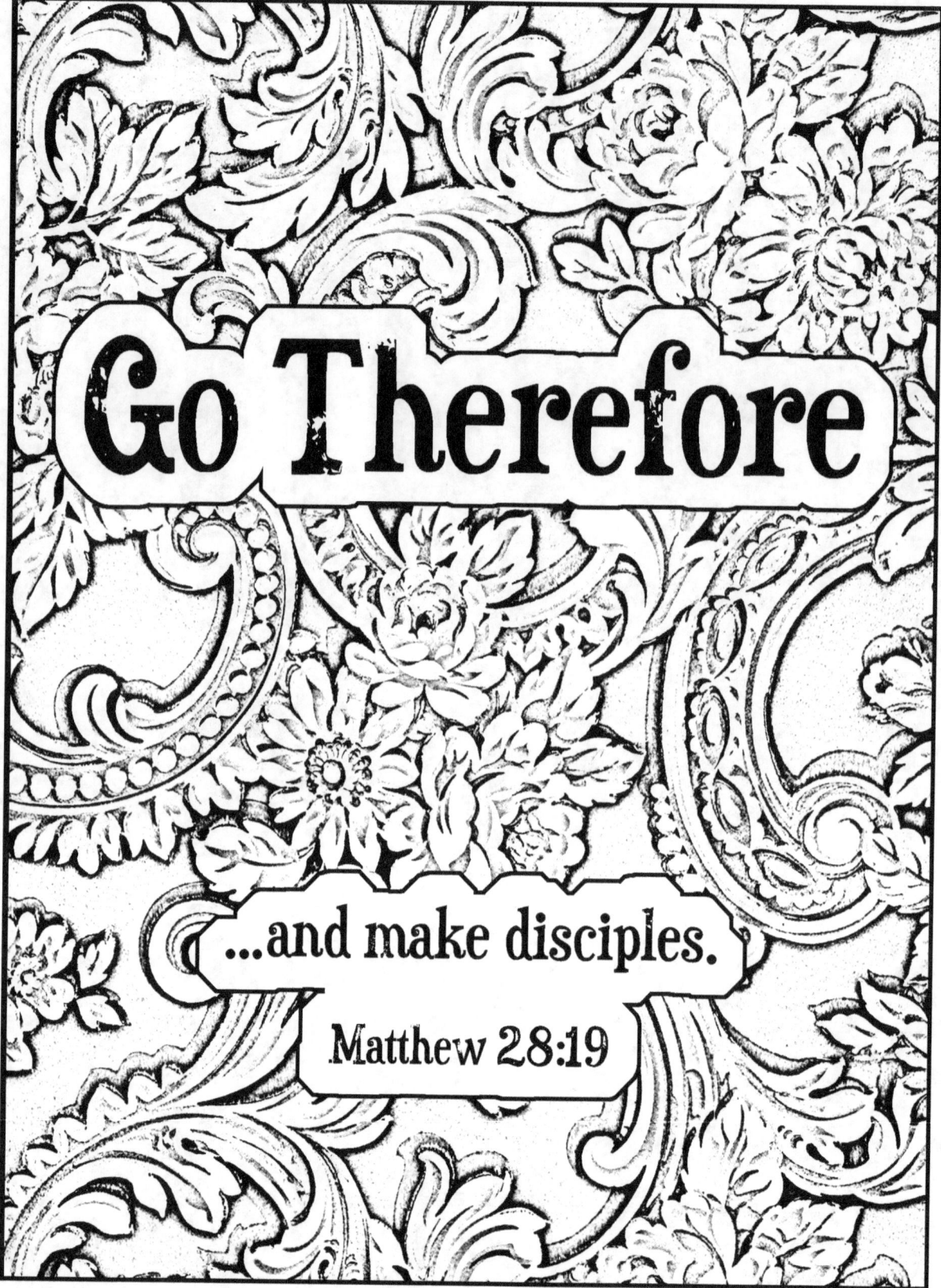

Go Therefore

...and make disciples.

Matthew 28:19

4 • A Hallelujah Sendoff!

Now that you have come this far, you have been fortified by knowledge and are ready for the task at hand—that is, to live the Christian life and proclaim the gospel of Jesus Christ. "That is why we always pray for you, asking our God to help you live the kind of life He called you to live. We pray that with His power God will help you do the good things you want and perform the works that come from your faith. We pray all this so that the name of our Lord Jesus Christ will have glory in you, and you will have glory in Him. That glory comes from the grace of our God and the Lord Jesus Christ."[1]

As you go forward in your new life in Christ Jesus, consider these special blessings that you now have:

God will never stop loving you. There is nothing you can do to lose God's love, just as there is nothing you can do to earn God's love. He loves you not

---

[1] 2 Thessalonians 1:11–12, New Century Version (NCV).

because of what you do or don't do but because of *who He is*. You are His forever, even when you fall short of your goals. Jesus said of His followers, "No one can snatch them away from Me, for My Father has given them to Me, and He is more powerful than anyone else. No one can snatch them from the Father's hand."[2]

> # God drew you to Himself and waited patiently for you to be ready to come to Him—He will surely see you through to the end.

God's very nature is one of patience and love. "The LORD is kind and merciful. He is patient and full of love."[3] God knows your strengths and your weaknesses and loved you before you loved Him. He drew you to Himself and waited patiently for you to be ready to come to Him—He will surely see you through to the end. "I am sure that the good work God began in you will continue until He completes it on the day when Jesus Christ comes again."[4]

God is rooting for you. "This message is from the LORD. 'I have good plans for you. I don't plan to hurt you. I plan to give you hope and a good future.'"[5] God does not desire to see you fail. He is not lying in wait for a chance to trick you or trip you up so He can punish you. That is not His nature. He wants you to succeed. He has good plans for you.

God sent His Holy Spirit to be with you and in you at all times. "I will ask the Father, and He will give you another Helper to be with you forever. The

---

[2] John 10:28–29, NLT.

[3] Psalm 103:8.

[4] Philippians 1:6.

[5] Jeremiah 29:11.

Helper is the Spirit of truth .... He lives with you, and He will be in you."[6] You have the still, small voice of God inside you in the form of His Holy Spirit, prompting you, guiding you into all truth, and helping you mature.

God gives you power. "The Spirit of God, who raised Jesus from the dead, lives in you."[7] This means you can do things by the power of God's Spirit that you could never do on your own. The disciples experienced this when "they were all filled with the Holy Spirit. Then they preached the Word of God with boldness."[8] With God's Holy Spirit within you, you now have that boldness too. "But the Holy Spirit will come on you and give you power. You will be My witnesses. You will tell people everywhere about Me."[9]

God has a new family for you. "Now you are no longer strangers to God and foreigners to heaven, but you are members of God's very own family, citizens of God's country, and you belong in God's household with every other Christian."[10] This means that you are now part of a spiritual family and a community of like-minded followers of Jesus. This is a community that spans the globe and the ages, but it is also local. There are probably people in your immediate area with whom you can meet, worship, learn, and grow.

---

[6] John 14:16–17.

[7] Romans 8:11, NLT.

[8] Acts 4:31, NLT.

[9] Acts 1:8.

[10] Ephesians 2:19, THE LIVING BIBLE (TLB).

God has eternity for you. Even when you are old and ready to pass from this world, you can look forward with hope toward an eternity in the presence of God. "Surely goodness and mercy shall follow me all the days of my life; and I will dwell in the house of the LORD forever." [11] Ever wonder what heaven will be like? The important thing about heaven is that you will be in God's presence, to behold Him and see His face. Like Moses, we will see Jesus "face to face," [12] and it will be awesome for eternity.

You can be sure of your salvation. How can you know that you are truly saved? Only Christianity offers believers the assurance of salvation. Your salvation is not based on anything you do or don't do but on who God is and His love for you. "If you openly say, 'Jesus is Lord' and believe in your heart that God raised Him from death, you will be saved." [13] Rest assured that God's Word is truth—He loves you and wants you to be where He is. Remember Jesus's words: "Father, I want these people You have given Me to be with Me in every place I am. I want them to see My glory—the glory You gave Me because You loved Me before the world was made." [14] No matter how you may feel or what circumstances you face, the truth of the Lord is unfailing love.

Can you think of other benefits of living the Christian life besides the blessings listed above? Discuss.

_____

_____

_____

_____

_____

_____

[11] Psalm 23:6, NKJV.

[12] Exodus 33:11.

[13] Romans 10:9.

[14] John 17:24.

Doing God's Will

God does not leave you to do your work alone. When you pray, fast, and seek His will in all you do, you prepare yourself for partnership with Him. You become a "worker who has no reason to be ashamed of his work, one who applies the true teaching in the right way."[15]

> # If God calls you to do something, He will also equip you to do it. He won't send you off to cross an ocean without providing a boat.

If God calls you to do something, He will also equip you to do it. He won't send you off to cross an ocean without providing a boat. That is not to say your ocean journey will be easy—God might want to stretch and grow you by allowing you to feel some big waves blow against you on the sea. He knows what you can handle better than you do. But rest assured, He will be with you. God will always be cheering you on from the pages of His book, the Holy Bible, and you will feel the promptings of His Holy Spirit within your spirit as you travel. He is the wind in your sails and the north star by which you navigate.

When you think about the "good works" that you will be called by God to do in your life, you may not know all the details of what exactly those works will be—each

[15] 2 Timothy 2:15.

individual has a different role to play and different talents to bring to God's tasks. But whatever they are, you will do them with love, remembering that you are an ambassador for Jesus. Sometimes you will have the opportunity to share the good news of what Jesus has done for you. Other times, your love for others and your behavior will be your gospel message. "You should be a light for other people. Live so that they will see the good things you do and praise your Father in heaven."[16]

As for seeking God's will, this is something you will learn to do at every turn in your Christian walk. To do the will of God is your highest goal. "Yes, it is God who is working in you. He helps you want to do what pleases Him, and He gives you the power to do it."[17]

You are asked to "always be ready to answer everyone who asks you to explain about the hope you have."[18] Some people will ask for you to give an answer for your faith because they are curious. Others may be hostile. Some may be confused. Others may feel rejected by your choice to follow Jesus. They will be friends, family, or strangers. They will be Muslims, atheists, cultists, Buddhists, Hindus, and Jews. Think about how will you explain the gospel in your own words.

James says, "Show me your faith without your works, and I will show you my faith by my works" (James 2:18). Read James 2:14-18 and discuss the connection between faith and works.

_____

_____

_____

_____

_____

---

[16] Matthew 5:16.

[17] Philippians 2:13.

[18] 1 Peter 3:15.

Your Testimony

Testimony: The declaration of a witness.

The apostle John once had a great vision of heaven, and he recorded it in the last book of the Bible, called the Revelation. During that vision, John learned of the day that is to come when the victory in the Great Battle between good and evil is finally won. The victory has already been won now, but we see it only in part. God's enemy still wanders the earth "like a roaring lion looking for someone to devour." [19] When Jesus returns, His victory will be complete. In John's vision, he sees a glimpse of that final day and explains: "And they [the believers in Jesus] have defeated him [the devil] by the blood of the Lamb and by their testimony." [20]

Notice there are two important tools that overcome the enemy of God in the Great Battle. One is "the blood of the Lamb." That is the work that only Jesus could do. He lay down His life as "the Lamb of God who takes away the sin of the world." [21] His shed blood gained us the victory. For this, we honor and praise God, who

---

[19] 1 Peter 5:8, NLT.

[20] Revelation 12:11, NLT.

[21] John 1:29, NLT.

redeemed us by "the precious blood of Christ, the sinless, spotless Lamb of God."[22]

The other tool John speaks of that helps in overcoming the enemy is the testimony of believers. Your testimony as a believer has power. It speaks of Jesus's victory over evil, sin, and death by drawing from your own undeniable experience of what God has done in your life. Your testimony is your story of Jesus's victory made personal to you, and it is powerful because it is true. It is the testimony that *you* can give.

In a court of law, witnesses give evidence to establish the truth in a case. If you are witness to a crime and are called up to give your testimony, you are expected to tell the truth. You might even have to "swear to tell the truth, the whole truth, and nothing but the truth, so help you God." Truth has value. Truth has power. The apostle Paul tells us that the gospel "is the power of God for salvation to everyone who believes."[23] The only way the gospel can have the power to save is that it is true. Falsehood does not have the power to save. Wild imaginings do not set you free. Only truth sets you free. Truth saves. Jesus calls Himself the Truth, and He calls the Holy Spirit the Spirit of Truth.

Your testimony about how Jesus has worked in your life to save you and sanctify you is powerful because it is about the most important truth for you—a truth that has everlasting, life-and-death consequences.

The Bible tells the story of a man born lame who was miraculously healed when the apostles Peter and John told him to rise in the name of Jesus. The rulers wanted Peter and John to stop preaching about Jesus because they were against Jesus. The rulers knew of this man and that he had been lame from birth, but the testimony that the man gave about being healed by Jesus was too powerful for them to oppose. "There was nothing that they [the rulers] could say, because they saw the man who had been healed standing there with Peter and John."[24]

---

[22] 1 Peter 1:19, NLT.

[23] Romans 1:16, ESV.

[24] Acts 4:14, GNT.

That lame man had a testimony about a miracle Jesus did in his life, and "there was nothing that they could say" because the man's healing was clear for everyone to see. The rulers could not deny the truth of what had happened to the man. That man's healing was his testimony.

You also have a personal testimony about what Jesus has done in your life. Others will benefit from hearing how God has touched your life in a way that is personal and unique to you. That is your story, and no one can take it away from you.

John the Baptist had a testimony: "He [John] came as a witness, to testify about the Light, so that all might believe through him."[25]

Why did John testify? "So that all might believe through him," and that is the reason for you to give your testimony as well.

Have you shared your testimony yet? What responses have you gotten from those you have shared it with?

_____

_____

_____

Planting Seeds

You do not have the power to save people. You might think of yourself as a farmer. It is your job to plant the seeds of the gospel and your testimony, and God takes it from there. The apostle Paul speaks about working

---

[25] John 1:7, CSB.

alongside one such spiritual farmer named Apollos: "I planted the seed and Apollos watered it. But God is the one who made the seed grow."[26]

With time, you will be able to stand and confidently deliver the message of the saving power of Jesus Christ and not be afraid, because you will be equipped with knowledge of the Word and the power of the Holy Spirit. You will be ready to stand and deliver your testimony to anyone. You will be ready to "go and make followers of all people in the world,"[27] as Jesus tells us to do in His Great Commission.

We ask the Lord to bless you with a life of love, holiness, sharing the good news, worship, purity, stewardship, and study. We pray that you will discover the joy of belonging to God's family and that the Bible's words will open up for you as a daily source of life, meaning, purpose, and comfort. We look forward to meeting you and celebrating Jesus with you as brothers and sisters in God's eternal kingdom one day.

"So then, my dear friends, stand firm and steady. Keep busy always in your work for the Lord, since you know that nothing you do in the Lord's service is ever useless."[28]

---

26 1 Corinthians 3:6.

27 Matthew 28:19.

28 1 Corinthians 15:58, GNT.

A Prayer

Here is a prayer you might wish to use as a pledge to declare to God your determination to follow Him and do His will:

Father God, You are my source of life. I pledge my hands, my heart, my mind, my mouth—all of me—as an instrument for You to use according to Your perfect will. I pledge my life to You. Fill me with Your Holy Spirit and give me boldness to proclaim Your gospel to the world and live a life of holiness and love. Help me to run the race as one completely set apart for Your purposes. Keep me from the snares of the enemy. Give me strength to run the race to the end so that I may one day hear You say, "Well done, My good and faithful servant." 29

29 Matthew 25:23, NLT.

More for You

Father's Love Letter

The words you are about to experience are true. They will change your life if you let them. For they come from the very heart of God. He loves *you*. And He is the Father you have been looking for all your life. This is His love letter to you.

My Child,

You may not know Me, but I know everything about you (Psalm 139:1).

I know when you sit down and when you rise up (Psalm 139:2).

I am familiar with all your ways (Psalm 139:3).

Even the very hairs on your head are numbered (Matthew 10:29–31).

For you were made in My image (Genesis 1:27).

In Me you live and move and have your being (Acts 17:28).

For you are My offspring (Acts 17:28).

I knew you even before you were conceived (Jeremiah 1:4–5).

I chose you when I planned creation (Ephesians 1:11–12).

You were not a mistake, for all your days are written in My book (Psalm 139:15–16).

I determined the exact time of your birth and where you would live (Acts 17:26).

You are fearfully and wonderfully made (Psalm 139:14).

I knit you together in your mother's womb (Psalm 139:13).

And brought you forth on the day you were born (Psalm 71:6).

I have been misrepresented by those who don't know Me (John 8:41–44).

I am not distant and angry, but am the complete expression of love (1 John 4:16).

And it is My desire to lavish My love on you (1 John 3:1).

Simply because you are My child and I am your Father (1 John 3:1).

I offer you more than your earthly father ever could (Matthew 7:11).

For I am the perfect father (Matthew 5:48).

Every good gift that you receive comes from My hand (James 1:17).

For I am your provider, and I meet all your needs (Matthew 6:31–33).

My plan for your future has always been filled with hope (Jeremiah 29:11).

Because I love you with an everlasting love. (Jeremiah 31:3).

My thoughts toward you are countless as the sand on the seashore (Psalm 139:17–18).

And I rejoice over you with singing (Zephaniah 3:17).

I will never stop doing good to you (Jeremiah 32:40).

For you are My treasured possession (Exodus 19:5).

I desire to establish you with all My heart and all My soul (Jeremiah 32:41).

And I want to show you great and marvelous things (Jeremiah 33:3).

If you seek Me with all your heart, you will find Me (Deuteronomy 4:29).

Delight in Me and I will give you the desires of your heart (Psalm 37:4).

For it is I who gave you those desires (Philippians 2:13).

I am able to do more for you than you could possibly imagine (Ephesians 3:20).

For I am your greatest encourager (2 Thessalonians 2:16–17).

I am also the Father who comforts you in all your troubles (2 Corinthians 1:3–4).

When you are brokenhearted, I am close to you (Psalm 34:18).

As a shepherd carries a lamb, I have carried you close to My heart (Isaiah 40:11).

One day I will wipe away every tear from your eyes (Revelation 21:3–4).

And I'll take away all the pain you have suffered on this earth (Revelation 21:3–4).

I am your Father, and I love you even as I love My son, Jesus (John 17:23).

For in Jesus, My love for you is revealed (John 17:26).

He is the exact representation of My being (Hebrews 1:3).

He came to demonstrate that I am for you, not against you (Romans 8:31).

And to tell you that I am not counting your sins (2 Corinthians 5:18–19).

Jesus died so that you and I could be reconciled (2 Corinthians 5:18–19).

His death was the ultimate expression of My love for you (1 John 4:10).

I gave up everything I loved that I might gain your love (Romans 8:31–32).

If you receive the gift of My son Jesus, you receive Me (1 John 2:23).

And nothing will ever separate you from My love again.(Romans 8:38–39).

Come home and I'll throw the biggest party heaven has ever seen (Luke 15:7).

I have always been Father, and will always be Father (Ephesians 3:14–15).

My question is … Will you be My child? (John 1:12–13).

I am waiting for you (Luke 15:11–32).

Love, *Your Dad.*
ALMIGHTY GOD

The Victorious Warrior

(Chorus) Vic- torious, vic- torious—, hear the gospel cry——. Vic-

torious, vic- torious—, the Son of God did rise——. With

power, might and glo— ry, the heavenly hosts a- gree—,

and the Victorious War- rior is walking next to me. (1) The

Victorious War- ri- or, His victory has been won———.

clothed in righteous glo—— ry, de- fender, Sav- ior, Son———, be-

fore the world, He knew me. In my heart He does a- bide———————. I'm not

fear- ful, I'm not shaken. I've got Je- sus by— my side. Vic-

Words and music by Jerry Shelfer © 2025 RaeLoch Publishing

(Verse 2)

My worth is all in Jesus. I'm the hidden pearl He found.

He said that I was wanted and the price He paid profound.

For everlasting life was His precious blood applied.

Now Jesus Christ, My Savior, is walking by my side.

(Verse 3)

Until my life is over and the coming of the Son,

When the dead in Christ have risen and the final battle's won,

Keep the faith proclaiming with the Bible as your guide,

And tell the world of victory with Jesus by your side.

Litany of Humility

Here is a prayer that many have found useful. It points to our need to be reminded of the correct posture we are to take as we come before God's throne of grace. The Bible tells us, "Do nothing out of selfish ambition or conceit, but in humility consider others as more important than yourselves."[1] This is one way we show love for one another, as Jesus commands us. Let this prayer challenge you to walk more and more each day like the One who describes Himself as "gentle and humble in spirit."[2]

O JESUS! MEEK AND HUMBLE OF HEART, HEAR ME.

From the desire of being esteemed, *Deliver me, Jesus.*

From the desire of being loved, *Deliver me, Jesus.*

From the desire of being extolled, *Deliver me, Jesus.*

From the desire of being honored, *Deliver me, Jesus.*

From the desire of being praised, *Deliver me, Jesus.*

From the desire of being preferred to others, *Deliver me, Jesus.*

From the desire of being consulted, *Deliver me, Jesus.*

From the desire of being approved, *Deliver me, Jesus.*

From the fear of being humiliated, *Deliver me, Jesus.*

From the fear of being despised, *Deliver me, Jesus.*

From the fear of suffering rebukes, *Deliver me, Jesus.*

From the fear of being calumniated [falsely charged], *Deliver me, Jesus.*

From the fear of being forgotten, *Deliver me, Jesus.*

From the fear of being ridiculed, *Deliver me, Jesus.*

From the fear of being wronged, *Deliver me, Jesus.*

From the fear of being suspected, *Deliver me, Jesus.*

---

[1] Philippians 2:3, CSB.

[2] Matthew 11:29.

That others may be loved more than I, *Jesus, grant me the grace to desire it.*

That others may be esteemed more than I, *Jesus, grant me the grace to desire it.*

That, in the opinion of the world, others may increase and I may decrease, *Jesus, grant me the grace to desire it.*

That others may be chosen and I set aside, *Jesus, grant me the grace to desire it.*

That others may be praised and I unnoticed, *Jesus, grant me the grace to desire it.*

That others may be preferred to me in everything, *Jesus, grant me the grace to desire it.*

That others may become holier than I, provided that I may become as holy as I should, *Jesus, grant me the grace to desire it.*

Amen![3]

---

[3] Various versions of this prayer have been used by the faithful for over a century.

Acknowledgments

We wish to thank those who made this book possible. Firstly, we thank the Author and Finisher of our faith, Jesus Christ, with and through whom all things are possible. We thank those students of the Victorious Warrior course who enthusiastically asked us for more. We thank those Kenyan partners who made clear to us that our work would be useful for discipling in their communities. We thank those Pakistani partners who are reaching thousands for Jesus in that mostly Muslim nation. Specifically, we thank Ivan Githinji, Missionary Keith Gafner, Pastor Joseph Muhoro, Silas Simotwa, Riziki Mueni, Catherine Bati, Pastor Shamaun Saad, Bishop Farooq Saad, Pastor Tom Lwanga Kawere of Uganda, Jingo Christopher, Godfrey Kalyesubula, Gema Cano, and the whole international Victorious Warrior teaching team. As you read this, more and more are joining the team, and our books are being translated into languages worldwide.

We thank those who took the time to read and give helpful guidance, including Michael Graham, Katie Philpott, Lesia Knudsen, Pastor Shamaun Saad, Missionary Keith Gafner, and Francis Saigut. Their thoughtful and excellent feedback and suggestions made this a better book.

We thank those who partner with us through prayer, great ideas, encouragement, teaching, and donations. They are invaluable in making this ministry possible.

Author Resources

AUTHORS JERRY AND MICHELLE SHELFER run a 501(c)(3) nonprofit called Prepare a Room Ministries, which offers the healing work of the cross to those hurt by abortion and the culture of death and disciples the next generation to embrace life and the Giver of life. This ministry can be found at:

VictoriousWarrior.org

PrepareaRoom.com

TheFoundlings.net

michelleshelfer.substack.com

@PrepareaRoom

THE VICTORIOUS WARRIOR:
Challenging Young People to Aim toward the Good
by Jerry and Michelle Shelfer

NOT LONG AGO, JUDEO-CHRISTIAN VALUES permeated many cultures of the world. This gave youths an identity grounded in a firm sense of right and wrong. Pursuit of excellence, love of truth, and serving others were values that were honored and led to good choices for the best outcomes in their young lives.

Today, young people are anxious and confused as they look to social media and other godless sources for identity, meaning, and direction. How are we to inspire them to make good choices for their best lives in a language that engages them—one they can claim as their own?

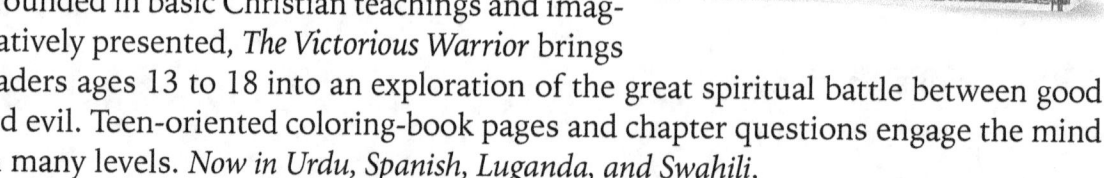

Grounded in basic Christian teachings and imaginatively presented, *The Victorious Warrior* brings readers ages 13 to 18 into an exploration of the great spiritual battle between good and evil. Teen-oriented coloring-book pages and chapter questions engage the mind on many levels. *Now in Urdu, Spanish, Luganda, and Swahili.*

PREPARE A ROOM:
A Path to Peace and Healing for Those Hurt by Abortion
by Michelle Shelfer

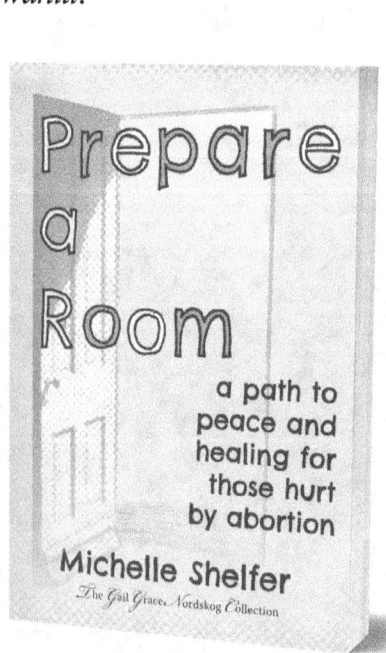

A CULTURE OF DENIAL about the traumatic effects of abortion has left many women and men trapped in regret, shame, and self-condemnation about their experience. Michelle Shelfer offers a ten-step path to peace and healing that addresses the damage done to identity and relationships and offers real-life tools to restore what has been broken. Embark on a journey that honors your unique story and opens the door to restoration through discovery of the greatest love.

Be a Part of the Victorious Warrior Mission!

The *Victorious Warrior* books are having an amazing impact on youths across the globe. You can see the testimonies of youths at VictoriousWarrior.org. We cannot do this without you. You can be a part of the Victorious Warrior outreach to youth by standing beside us with prayer and with your giving. If you wish to make a tax-deductible donation, please find your options below. If you have donations of other than cash and cars, please contact Jerry at jerry@ preparearoom.com.

- **Paypal and Zelle**: Michelle@PrepareaRoom.com
- **Venmo**: @Prepare-a-Room
- **Donate a car** for a tax deduction at GiveCars4Life.com

Michelle Shelfer
@Prepare-a-Room

venmo

PayPal

Give Cars 4 Life

www.ingramcontent.com/pod-product-compliance
Lightning Source LLC
Chambersburg PA
CBHW080901120626
46555CB00008B/2907